Praise for *Happy Kids Happy You*

As a father of five children, I loved *Happy Kids Happy You*. I just wished I'd had Sue's guidance when I began my journey as a parent but hey it's never too late to learn. As an NLP practitioner, I recognised Sue's advice as good NLP practice and she has a wonderfully accessible way of putting the message across. Not only did I pick up great tips on relating to children, I also found myself thinking how much I could apply with adults too. Sue's key lessons are delivered in inspirational bite-sized chunks and I just love all the mini case studies she has gleaned from other parents. This has got to be essential reading for every mum and dad. In fact I reckon there should be a copy provided by the state for every birth registered. It would make the world a much better place. Thank you Sue.

Clive Wilson
Deputy Chairman, Primeast, Specialist in leadership, change and teamwork

++++

As a working mum with four children under eleven I SO need this book! Sue makes it all extremely relatable and gives really positive practical suggestions for dealing with "spirited" children in all kinds of situations from the frustrations of getting ready to go out to really challenging behaviour. I've tried some of her strategies and already I'm noticing the difference. A really useful inspirational guide.

Janey Lee Grace
Author of Imperfectly Natural Woman, www.imperfectlynatural.com

++++

I was delighted to see Sue's techniques and tips in print. Sue has provided training workshops for our service, both for a mum's support group and for volunteers working with children. Sue gives us tools and techniques to help with the myriad sticky situations of parenting – to help us keep our cool when tempers get hot, to communicate effectively with our children and, most of all, enjoy those precious years. I have tried out a number of Sue's methods with my grandchild AND they do work!

Lizzie Evans
Manager of Mums in Need of Support, RGN, Dip. Couns, BA Sociology, MA Health Service Studies

I have read through *Happy Kids Happy You* with two hats, first and foremost from a parent/grandparent view and the second from a childcarer view.

Having two children of my own (both adults now) views on behaviour were very different to what they are today; being a new grandparent has shown me just how much this change has been.

Being in childcare for the past 20+ years the one area that I am constantly asked about is behaviour management. Comments such as 'Oh he just won't listen' or 'Why won't she do as she is told?' are questions I am always asked. Reading Sue's book certainly captures all of these comments and with clear tips and examples shows how to react in a clear calm and most of all positive way.

The book makes you think of different situations you have found yourself in: I heard myself saying "I can relate to that, that's what happened when ..." During training as a nursery manager we were always told to back a negative situation with a positive. This reflects through the whole of the book showing parents or carers that developing new techniques can help to achieve good results with parents and children working together.

One area I particularly like is 'Concentrate on something mundane' - this puts everything into perspective for me. When at work if things are getting tense I have a photograph of my grandson on my desk and by looking at him takes all of the tension away; two minutes of 'time out' allows me to calm down and get on track for the next challenge.

The book shows a fun way of helping parents achieve their goals. If this book was given to every new parent I am sure challenging behaviour would be less of an issue.

When children commence nursery we open a file called 'My Learning Journey'. Reading Sue's book relates to these profiles and I would class the book as a 'Learning Journey' for parents. If parents/carers are calm, positive and most of all happy in their approach, then this can only have a positive effect on our children.

The title of the book is *Happy Kids Happy You* - it portrays that happy parents help to make happy children. We are the teachers and children will copy everything we do. A learning journey that never ends.

A very clear, informative and practical book to have in any home or workplace. I will certainly be recommending it to all my parents.

Joyce Forster
Head of First Steps Nursery, Harrogate

Sue Beever

Happy Kids Happy You

Using **NLP** to bring out the best
in ourselves and the children we care for

Crown House Publishing Ltd
www.crownhouse.co.uk
www.crownhousepublishing.com

First published by

Crown House Publishing Ltd
Crown Buildings, Bancyfelin, Carmarthen, Wales, SA33 5ND, UK
www.crownhouse.co.uk

and

Crown House Publishing Company LLC
6 Trowbridge Drive, Suite 5, Bethel, CT 06801, USA
www.crownhousepublishing.com

First Published 2009. Reprinted 2009, 2011

British Library of Cataloguing-in-Publication Data
A catalogue entry for this book is available from the British Library.

Print ISBN 978-184590128-8
Mobi ISBN 978-184590322-0
ePub ISBN 978-184590323-7
LCCN 2008936751

Printed and bound in the UK by
Bell & Bain Ltd, Glasgow

This book is dedicated to you.

May you find something of relevance and use in helping you
to bring out the best in yourself and the children you care for.

CONTENTS

SECTION 3: Take care of YOU

SECTION 4: Enjoy the journey

The journey continues

Starting Out

Welcome to

Having children is an opportunity for creating and enjoying greater happiness in the world. And yet, sometimes our children's behaviour drives us to distraction! Why is it that the things we try to do for the best often backfire, giving us the opposite of what we wanted?

When it comes to parenting, whilst we may sometimes wish for a magic wand or at least a consistent formula for getting it right, there is no such thing. So this book is not about coming up with the right answers all the time and how to be a "perfect parent". This book is about being the best *real parent* you can be, moment by moment, by choosing to use *what works* in good communication. Adopting effective ways to relate to your children can enhance your children's lives and your own, resulting in more happiness all round. This book shows you how to do this.

Many of us come to parenting with high expectations of what life *should* be like. The reality can be very different: our lives are increasingly busy as we try to meet not only our own needs but those of our children and families, as well as all our other responsibilities. Little wonder it's so easy to notice when our expectations are not being met. We notice more and more of the behaviour we **don't** want from our children.

With the best of intentions, what we then say or do can often make things worse. We get even more of what we **don't** want!

The truth is, you're doing the best you can in any given situation, with the choices you have available to you at that moment:

SITUATION + YOU + Your CHOICES ⇒ RESULT i.e.

What happens next

The methods in this book are all about giving yourself more choices, more options – more ways of thinking and doing something *that works* so that:

- you get great results with your children
- your life goes more smoothly
- you feel more confident and positive
- you have fun and enjoy being a parent more of the time!

Your children need you!

When it comes to parenting, there are no right answers, no universal solutions, no absolute truths. There is only the here and now of what is going to work for you and your children, moment by moment, on *your* parenting journey. You are the expert on your family and your children. You are in the front line. No matter how well intentioned the advice of others, it's you who must decide … and you who must live with the consequences.

So it makes sense to find out about *what works* in good communication. With methods that work and a little practice, you only need a moment, a **pause for thought**, to then choose to:

- Say or do something useful
- Encourage behaviour that you **do** want: behaviour that is positive and useful for you and your children.

You're then creating the kind of relationships, family life and future that you **do** want for yourself, your children and your children's children.

This book focuses on your needs – **Happy You** – as well as the needs of your children – **Happy Kids**. You are a significant part of the equation and have a major effect on the results you get. So family life has to work for you as well as the children you care for. And to help and encourage you along the way, you'll find many examples of how people just like you have used these methods to find solutions that worked for them.

How to use this book

The methods are presented in a consistent and easy-to-read format. Each method starts with an introduction which is followed by details of the **method**. Then there are one or two **examples**, followed by **tips for good results** when using the method. **Now you have a go** gives you ways of practising the method **and finally** … gives closing thoughts about the method. **How this method worked for** … gives examples of how others have used the method to good effect.

A clock symbol at the beginning of each method suggests how much time you need to get an idea of the method and to start using it. For example

5 minutes   15 minutes

A mirror symbol indicates that a level of reflection is required: some calm time out, to think about and get the hang of the method.

The methods are grouped into sections and ordered with the easiest first as each method builds on the previous methods through each section of the book.

Each method is self-contained so you can simply **dip** into whichever method appeals to you, depending on the current challenges you face and the time you have available. The **Quick reference guide** in **Appendix I** gives suggestions for where to start with some common types of challenge. References to specific behaviours can be found in the **Index**.

Alternatively, you can start at the beginning of the book and **take more time** to work your way through the sections and methods as they are presented. Reading this way gives you the experience of progressing through the methods, with earlier methods often adding to your use and understanding of later methods.

And of course, you can do both.

Dipping

Getting a "quick fix" while you're in the thick of caring for your children can reassure you that you're not alone or simply help you draw breath. Keep this book easily accessible so that you can dip into it whenever you need a moment of calm and you'll be able to return to the fray with a smile on your face! The book can also give you a new idea or perspective on a tricky situation that has just happened or is about to happen. You can use the fact that you feel less than happy about it to motivate you to dip into a method and find new ways of dealing with it for next time … because, one way or another, there's always a next time, isn't there?!

Taking more time

Taking more thoughtful and calm "time out" to work through the methods and become really familiar with them will help you recognise and take opportunities to use them. It will also help you prepare how you will use a method for a particular recurring "hot spot" situation or behaviour.

Familiarity and practice also builds your flexibility in any situation, so that you can try out methods and go with what's working. Remember, there is no right answer; it's about finding what's going to work to get the result you want for the situation you are in. The method that worked well last week may not work this week; situations change as your children grow, learn and adapt. With increasing choice and flexibility, if the first method you try doesn't fit, you'll simply move on to another.

The more methods you know, the more options you have.

Here's an overview of the methods you'll find in each section:

Section 1: In the moment – *words and behaviour to keep things running smoothly*
Methods to help you **do** something different with your words and actions *in the moment*.

Turn Don'ts into Do's

Turn Stop's into Go's

Offer effective choices

Get a "Yes!"

Be impressed!
Give praise the *EASY* way

Get down to their level

Move beside

Join them in their activity

Section 2: More challenging situations – *different thinking opens up new ways forward*
Methods that give you ways to **think** differently in *more challenging situations*.

 **What you focus on
is what you get**

**Set and maintain
reasonable boundaries**

 **Give and take: the
dance of responsibility**

**Find a useful
meaning**

 **Clean up
your thinking**

**Find out what your
body knows**

Section 3: Take care of *YOU* – *being the best you can be for yourself and your children*
How to **be** different, more resourceful and in a better mood more of the time,
by *taking care of YOU*. When you're in a better mood it's much easier to think and
behave more effectively. The methods are:

 **Pause for thought**

**Concentrate on
something mundane**

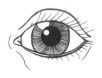 **Use peripheral vision**

**Give yourself praise
the *EASY* way**

**Celebrate your
successes daily**

You're doing
great!

**Give yourself a
good talking to**

**Balance your needs
into the mix**

Adjust your expectations

Section 4: Enjoy the journey – *learning from and with your children*
These methods demonstrate the benefits of **learning** alongside your children on
your parenting journey. They give you ways to learn with and from your children
to *enjoy the journey* more.

Walk your talk

It's cool to copy!

How was it for you?

**Practice makes
permanent**

Practice makes permanent

As you become familiar with these methods, the more you practise and try them out in different situations, the more they will become second nature to you. You'll notice that not only is your attitude to being a parent changing but also that the atmosphere in your home is so much better!

Share what works

You'll know from observing your children that sharing experiences is an exciting part of learning. As you make changes using the methods in this book, you may want to share your experiences with others and find out how they approach situations. The more people you share with, the more ideas you'll get! **Happy Kids Happy You** practice groups and workshops provide a safe and supportive environment for practising methods and sharing what works with others. There's more about **sharing what works** later in the book (page 221) and you'll find more information on workshops, practice groups, events and community on the website

www.happykids-happyyou.co.uk

This book will guide and support you in exploring more effective ways of relating to and communicating with your children towards more **Happy Kids Happy You**.

Enjoy the journey!

The examples in this book are intended to demonstrate how to apply the methods. They are not intended to be taken as giving specific advice for particular situations, although this does not stop you from using them as you deem appropriate for you and your children. The ages of children in examples are not always specified: most are in the range 1–8 years. Please adapt these examples to situations and contexts that are meaningful to you and your children.

From one parent to another...

Picture this:

It's mealtime and my toddler is throwing food on the floor. "Don't throw your food on the floor!" I say. He continues to throw food with even more enthusiasm!

And this:

My toddler and I are mixing cake mix together. As she lifts the spatula to her lips, I say, "Don't lick the spatula!" She shoves it in her mouth with a grin.

And this:

I'm preparing breakfast and I want my children to come and sit up at the table. I say to them, "It's time for breakfast. Come and sit up now please." Their response: "No!" One even adds, "I don't want any breakfast!" Before I know it, I have a fight on my hands.

And this:

My toddler keeps trying to kick me as we're doing a nappy change. This has been going on for a few days now and really annoys me. "Stop kicking me!" I say firmly, sternly even. To my increasing annoyance, I get kicked even more!

And this:

I need to get my toddler and young baby washed and ready for bed. "Let's go upstairs now," I say to my toddler, as I move towards the stairs. She rushes ahead of me and then sits down on the stairs right in front of me. Here we go again! She keeps doing this to get my attention, even though it's my anger and frustration, because I'm carrying the baby and can't see what I'm treading on. "We don't play on the stairs. Walk up the stairs properly!" I demand. She folds her arms, with a defiant "No!" This sets the tone for an unpleasant time ahead in the bathroom.

Do these sound familiar?

My life as a parent

Parenting was and continues to be *the most challenging thing I've ever done!* Before **Happy Kids Happy You**, when I regularly found myself in situations like these, I would get cross and frustrated with my children and ultimately with myself. I knew that what I was doing wasn't working: it wasn't getting the result I wanted and often seemed to make things worse. And I didn't like myself for what I was saying and doing, day in day out … but I didn't know what else to do. I seemed to be saying "No!" all the time, shouting and "losing it", focusing on the negatives and feeling guilty.

I would get plenty of advice from books, friends and family about *what to do regarding my child* in particular situations – and much of it was contradictory! However, nothing was helping me to *think more usefully for myself*. I wanted to become more confident and competent as a parent, to feel more in control, at least of myself! I wanted something better, something more useful and sustainable for myself and my children.

So I set out to learn more about *what works* in personal effectiveness, communication and relationships. I obviously had an instinctive, unconscious understanding of this, as we all do, having made it this far in life. However, now I wanted to become more consciously aware of what worked so that I could use it in family life, for my own good and for the good of my family. I read yet more books and eventually trained in neuro-linguistic progamming (NLP) (see Appendix II) which focuses on getting the results you want, especially using language and behaviour to positively influence those around you. It had an immediate and major impact on my life for the better.

It continues to shape the way I go about things, particularly how I think about and communicate with my children. I now have more choices about how I respond to situations that challenge me. I can communicate more usefully and respectfully to get the results I want more of the time. I can enforce boundaries more respectfully and kindly. And my children and I now have more fun more of the time.

Because these methods have made such a difference for me, I have created **Happy Kids Happy You**, to share these methods for bringing out the best in ourselves and the children we care for. I coach and train others in **Happy Kids**

Happy You methods through workshops, coaching, practice groups … and I'm delighted to be working with you now through this book. The methods in this book will help you to find solutions that work for you, right now.

So what's different?

Little changes can make a big difference. Let's go back to the previous situations and see how *Happy Kids Happy You* methods were used to keep the situation on an even keel and achieve a good result – when it could so easily have gone the other way. You'll be able to spot the methods when you've read more of this book.

- It's mealtime and my toddler is throwing food on the floor. I ignore this and say "Mmmm. Yummy food! We eat food, like this …" as I put a piece in my mouth. "Put that piece in your mouth …" I say encouragingly as I point to some food. To my amazement, he does! He chews and grins. "Let's eat some more food!" I say, as we start to enjoy eating our food together. **Result!**

- My toddler and I are mixing cake mix together. As she lifts the spatula to her lips, I say "Hey, keep mixing please!" She pauses, which gives me time to add, "You are mixing really, really well! Well done!" She smiles, puts the spatula back in the mix and gets mixing again. **Result!**

- I'm preparing breakfast and I want my children to come and sit up at the table. I say to them, "OK, would you like to choose where to sit today or are you just going to sit in your usual places?" As they both rush to the table, one says, "I want to sit next to you today!" to which the other says, "So do I!" "That's great!" I say as I move their chairs to either side of me. They both sit up with enthusiasm. **Result!**

- My toddler keeps trying to kick me as we're doing a nappy change. This has been going on for a few days now and really annoys me. This time, as I see a kick coming, I decide to treat it like a game and I snatch the leg in a playful way and say, "Atchacha!" This confuses my toddler and the next kick is much more tentative. I again snatch it saying "Atchacha!" and we giggle a bit together. It doesn't happen again.

Result!

● I need to get my toddler and young baby washed and ready for bed. "Let's go upstairs now," I say to my toddler, as I move towards the stairs. She rushes ahead of me and then sits down on the stairs right in front of me. I'm about to say the usual "We don't play on the stairs …" when I realise this isn't getting the result I want – a cooperative and happy time getting ready for bed. So I stop and sit down beside her on the stair. I don't say anything and simply wait. After a few moments, she looks at me and smiles. I smile back … then she just gets up and walks up the stairs!

Result!

Parenting continues to be the most challenging thing I've ever done. I still occasionally lose it and mess up … but less often. The difference is that now I accept this is part of being human, living and growing with children.

Let's begin this journey so that you can explore ways of **bringing out the best in yourself and the children you care for**.

Section 1

In the moment

Words and behaviour
to keep things running smoothly

In the moment

Introduction

This section gives you methods for saying and doing useful things in the moment, to get and keep things running smoothly. These quick and easy techniques offer ways to stay on top of everyday niggles and irritations, so that you feel more in control, calmer, happier and more positive. And this, in turn, will give you more energy and head space to deal with the more challenging situations which are explored in Section 2.

These are quick methods: in less than 5 minutes, you will be able to turn a **don't** into a **do**!... a **stop** into a **go**! They are easy to apply and immediately make a huge difference.

The first methods show you how to use words that work to say something useful.

The methods are:

- Turn Don'ts into Do's
- Turn Stop's into Go's
- Offer effective choices
- Get a "Yes!"
- Be impressed! Give praise the *EASY* way.

What we say

Teatime! Come down now. please!

from the bottom of the stairs

Come and sit up for breakfast.

from the kitchen

It's time to go now. Come on.

COME ON!

from the door

What kids hear

Blah Blah Blah Blah Blah Blah

The methods that follow give you ways of **doing** something different, using your behaviour and body language to connect well with your child so that your message gets through.

The methods are:

• Get down to their level
• Move beside
• Join them in their activity.

Don't lick the spoon!

Turn Don'ts into Do's

Whatever you're doing at the moment, don't look behind you … don't even think about what's going on behind you. Hard isn't it?! I bet, even if you didn't actually turn to look behind you, you were tempted to do so, and that's exactly what I asked you not to do! Now try this: don't think of a big grey elephant, with its long trunk swinging.

The reason you find it hard not to do what I've asked you not to do is because of how your brain works out what words mean. To understand not doing something, it seems the brain first creates an impression of what it is we're not meant to do. This impression can influence us to actually do it. Hypnotists use this language pattern, the "negative command", to give hypnotic suggestions to their clients. We are adults who have plenty of experience of language and what words mean. Now think what it's like for your child, who is just learning language and what words mean. Chances are you'll get more of exactly what you didn't want:

What you say	What they "hear"	What's likely to happen
Don't throw your food!	Throw your food!	Child thinks, "Sure thing!" and throws more food.
Stop smearing your yoghurt!	Smear your yoghurt!	Child thinks, "Wow, so this is called smearing yoghurt! It sounds as good as it feels!" as more is smeared.
Don't take your nappy off!	Take your nappy off!	Child proceeds to take off nappy.
Don't hit me!	Hit me!	Ouch!

In the moment

The method

Whenever you hear yourself thinking or saying, "Don't ...", "Stop ...", "You can't ...", or "You shouldn't ...", ask yourself:

What can I usefully and safely encourage my child to do instead?

Then tell your child what you want them to do. Use clear and simple words to offer them this alternative. Make it sound vivid and appealing to grab their attention and interest. Remember, their brain will create an impression of your suggestion, based on how well you've described it to them.

Here are some examples:

Don't

Don't talk with your mouth full!

Don't run on the road!

Don't just help yourself from the biscuit tin!

Do

Tell me when you've swallowed that mouthful ... Then I can hear you better.

Walk on the pavement!

You can help yourself to fruit or juice.

or

It's nearly teatime. Help me lay the table, then you can eat your tea as soon as it's ready.

Tips for good results

✓ It's OK to tell your child what you don't want them to do as long as you follow this up straight away with what you do want them to do instead.

✓ Whenever it's appropriate, reinforce your words with a clear demonstration of the behaviour you want, e.g. "We eat yoghurt like this …" followed by a clear demonstration of you spooning your yoghurt into your mouth. With young children, you can help them to do what you are requesting, e.g. help them to spoon their yoghurt into their mouth.

✓ **Turning Don'ts into Do's** is a great way to teach your child relevant, useful behaviour, when and where it's appropriate. If you're struggling to come up with an appropriate Do, ask yourself:

What do I do in this situation?

It may be useful to show and tell your child to do the same. Kate explains how this worked for her at the end of this section (page 31).

✓ At certain times, children (and teenagers) respond really well to a **prove me wrong** challenge. To do this, start to explain what you want your child to do with a challenge, something like:

"I bet you can't …"
or "I'm not sure you can …"

Your child then defiantly does what you want them to do to **prove you wrong**. You then need to be *really* impressed with what they've just done! For example:

"I bet you can't put all those clothes on before I've cleaned my teeth."
Followed by:
"Wow! You're all dressed! You put all your clothes on by yourself! Well done!"

Use **prove me wrong** with care. You'll get an immediate sense of whether you're going to get a good response. If not, use another method.

Now you have a go

Cover up the **Do's** with your hand or a piece of paper until you've thought of some **Do's** of your own to counter each of the **Don'ts**. When you're done, look at the suggestions for **Do's**.

Don't	**Do**

Don't be so rough with the baby!

Touch the baby really gently … like a fairy touch …

Stop turning the light on and off!

Leave the light on please! Look, now we can see what we're doing …

Don't fall off! [Child walking on wall]

You're balancing really well! Go steady …

Don't play on the stairs!

Play in here please … there's lots more room

Don't take such a big spoonful!

Take a normal spoonful so you can eat it easily

Stop! You'll break it!

Hold that really carefully … Put it down here …

Remember, there are no right answers. There is only what could work to get a useful result for you and your children in your current situation.

And finally …

Yes, you are probably using this method already, though you may call it something like distraction! The difference is that now you can understand why and how it works. If you only tell your children what you don't want them to do they'll get confused and are likely to show their frustration. It is far better to offer them things they can do.

I used to think it was important for my children to know exactly what they shouldn't do. I'm really glad I've moved on from that! In our society, we soon find out what we shouldn't be doing (see the introduction to the **Set and maintain reasonable boundaries** method, page 89), despite the fact that it's usually much more useful to know what we can do instead.

How this method worked for …

Hilary
In the supermarket, I used to say "don't run off" to my little boy. I instantly got a much better behaviour when I told him to "stay close to the trolley".
Result!

Kate
My children were waving their knives and forks around at mealtimes. I told them to put them down on their plates when they weren't using them but this didn't seem to help much.
  *When I asked myself **"What do I do in this situation?"** I realised I rarely put my cutlery down: I was busy loading my fork with my next mouthful. When I told my kids to do this too I got a better result – less waving of cutlery and they were more focused on eating.*
Result!

Lou
*I really try to focus on the **do's** and trying to think very quickly about rephrasing things more positively to get the outcome I want rather than immediately saying **don't**, which I was very guilty of doing.*
  My son really responds to me speaking more positively with him and I have noticed a different atmosphere in the home, much more positive and a lot calmer. Instead of yelling at him, "Don't speak to me like that," I now say, "Mummy will listen when you speak nicely," and it seems to win every time!
Result!

Turn Stop's into Go's

I was shocked one day when my eldest showed me the teeth marks on her arm where her 15-month-old sister had just bitten her. I'd heard that other children had been known to bite but I had naively and rather smugly thought that no child of mine would do such a thing … until they did! I knew that drawing attention to this behaviour with, "Don't bite! We don't bite in this house!" would lead to more of the same unless I followed it up with a clear Do (see **Turn Don'ts to Do's** method, page 27). But I was at a loss as to what Do would work in this situation!

When she sank her teeth into the back of my shoulder the following day as I was carrying her, I realised (through the exquisite pain!) that I needed to give her something else to bite!

The principle of **turning a Stop into a Go** is that no behaviour is of itself bad. What makes it unacceptable is the situation or timing of the behaviour, or the way it is being carried out.

Bizarre as it may sound, whenever my youngest then tried to bite me or anyone else, my response was, "Oh, you want to bite do you? Here, bite this…" and I would give her an apple or a carrot to bite on. I would encourage her to bite it and reinforce this behaviour with, "We bite food when we eat. Here is some food for you to eat." Of course, she was rarely actually hungry and was surprised and distracted by the sudden appearance of food. It seemed to work though, as she quickly got bored with this and stopped biting people.

The method

When you want your child to **Stop** doing something, ask yourself:

When, where or how might it be acceptable for them to do this?

Then, tell your child
- **where** they need to go to do it
- **when** they can do it
- **how** they can do it.

Here are some examples:

Stop!

Stop shouting!

Don't draw on there!
[wall, table, book …]

Stop what you're
doing now.

Go!

That's too loud for inside!
Do you want to be loud
and shout? You can shout
outside …

Oh, you want to do some
drawing? Here, come and
draw on this paper …

You can finish that
off after tea.

Tips for good results

✓ When you turn **Stop's** into **Go's**, what often happens is that your child gets bored with the unacceptable behaviour and doesn't bother doing it any more. This is because they're not getting lots of negative attention for it!

✓ When you first start turning **Stop's** into **Go's**, you may feel that you are offering your children some rather bizarre choices! It certainly took my child by surprise the first time I gave her an apple after she bit me. The key is to notice how effective your response is in getting the result you want: does it get you less of the unacceptable behaviour?

✓ Draw attention to acceptable behaviour when it occurs under normal circumstances, such as taking bites of food at mealtimes or giving a ball a good kick at a playing field. This helps your child associate the behaviour with the context in which it is appropriate.

Now you have a go

In the following table, cover up the last two columns with your hand or a piece of paper. Think of where, when and how the behaviours in the left hand column would be (i) unacceptable and (ii) acceptable to you. When you've come up with your own ideas, check out the suggestions given.

Behaviour	Unacceptable time and place	Acceptable time and place
Example: Shouting	At the meal table: "Stop shouting! That's too loud at the meal table"	In the hall: "If you want to shout, go in the hall. You can shout in the hall …"
Spitting	In general, anywhere except the bathroom	The bathroom
Jumping	On the sofa	On a cushion on the floor
Tearing paper	In books	Tearing tissue paper for craft work, e.g. for gluing and sticking
Standing on a chair	At mealtimes	To reach something up high
Throwing	Inside and especially at mealtimes	Outside for some playtime

In the moment

And finally ...

Telling children what they can't do builds resistance and ultimately resentment. Telling children what they can do (including when, where and how they can do it as necessary) encourages and reinforces appropriate behaviour. It also nurtures a "**can do**" approach to life!

How this method worked for ...

Tony

It was the end of a long day. I was talking to my 4-year-old daughter and she was asking if we could go swimming now. It was late at night, I was tired, it was literally five minutes before her bedtime and I wanted to blurt out, "What! What do you mean you want to go swimming now?!"

I had enough presence of mind (just) to pause and, when she spotted me hesitating, she said, "That's all right Daddy, we can do it another day can't we? We'll see if we have time tomorrow." I was amused and delighted to notice that she can turn Stop's into Go's too!
Result!

Jenna

I love the way this method enables me to transform unacceptable behaviour and requests from my children into a way forward that we can agree on. I feel much more reasonable and calm approaching situations in this way.

Practising turning Don'ts into Do's and Stop's into Go's, I now find I often ask myself, "How can I say Yes to this?" whenever I am about to say "No". This gives me the opportunity to come up with more useful ways forward than my straight "No" would have done.
Result!

When you just know they're going to say "No!"

The list goes on ... And don't you find that the more you *really* want them to wash or dress, the more you *urgently need* them to put their shoes and coats on or get in the car then the more likely they are to dig their heels in, saying "No!" with passion and determination! It's easy to feel that the battle lines are drawn and a confrontation or stand-off is inevitable.

It doesn't have to be like this! Here are two quick and easy methods for getting through the routine stuff and everyday tasks as quickly and easily as possible.

- Offer effective choices
- Get a "Yes".

Offer effective choices

2

Babies are completely dependent on their carers to interpret and meet their needs. As they grow up and become better able to express themselves, saying "No!" is a simple and powerful way for children to make themselves known, to try to take some control over what's happening to them and to express their preferences.

Being offered a choice, however small, gives a sense of involvement: that your wants and needs are being considered, respected and valued. It's good for all of us! Children are no different but they don't often get to choose much in the general scheme of things. Making a choice gives a child the opportunity to:

- take some control over what's happening to them

- recognise and develop their independence, as they generally choose to do more for themselves

- develop their sense of responsibility for themselves and their actions.

Undoubtedly you will already be offering your child choices in one way or another. The trick is understanding how to construct an *effective* choice that:

- engages your child, respects them and their needs – **Happy Kids**

- gets the result you need – **Happy You.**

The method

Assume that your child will do what you want them to do. Their choice will be about *how* they do it, not what they will do.

Don't even mention what needs to be done. Chances are they know full well what needs to happen and telling them will only increase their resistance. Think about it: how much do you like being told exactly what to do when you know anyway and maybe you were just about to do it?!

Offer a choice that enables your child to decide something about *how* to do what needs to be done.

Here are some examples:

The task

Choices

Time to get dressed now

Would you like to get dressed now? ✗

Would you like to choose your clothes today or shall I? ✓

Assumes your child is going to get dressed

Breakfast time! Come and sit up!

Would you like to sit up now? ✗

Would you like to sit next to me or Daddy today? ✓

Assumes your child is going to sit up for breakfast

Coats and shoes on now please

Shall we put our coats and shoes on now? ✗

Shall we put coats or shoes on first today? ✓

Assumes you and your child will put your coats and shoes on

Tips for good results

✓ Offer simple and clearly worded choices. Children need to understand what's being offered.

✓ Offer choices that are appropriate to your children's current preferences and abilities. Then they are more likely to enjoy what they are doing and succeed at it, and this motivates them to do it again.

✓ If you have a preference which option you would like your child to take, put your preferred option last. The last thing we say tends to have a greater impact so they are more likely to choose it.

This really made me think about how I say things. When I ran out of more useful methods, my ultimatum had often been: "Do you want to do this the easy way or the hard way?" i.e. happy, cooperative and fun *or* un-cooperative, strict and grumpy! I've changed this around now to: "Do you want to do this the hard way or the easy way?" The easy way sounds much more appealing and is easily the preferred choice!

A note of caution: although this sequence can be effective, there is no guarantee that people will choose the last option. For example, a very effective choice can be to ask a child if they want to do something themselves or have it done for them. They usually want to do it themselves, so something like, "Do you want to squeeze the toothpaste or shall I?" can often get a child to undertake the task with a defiant independence – in this case, cleaning their teeth.

✓ Make sure that all the choices you offer are OK for you. Only offer choices that you're happy for your child to take!

In the moment

✓   Notice what your child is doing. You can often use this in a simple choice that has the added benefit of validating and acknowledging them and their current activity. For example:

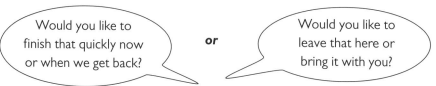

Would you like to finish that quickly now or when we get back?   *or*   Would you like to leave that here or bring it with you?

Both assume that you are leaving and your child is coming too!

Now you have a go

Look at the tasks in the thought bubbles on the left hand side. Think of an effective choice you could offer to get the task done. There are many possible ways of doing this, so cover up the suggestions on the right hand side until you have come up with one of your own. Remember there are no right answers; your suggestion is probably more likely to work with your child.

Time to go to bed   →   Would you like a Maisy or a Thomas story tonight? [in bed]

Get in the car please   →   Would you like to clip yourself into your car seat or shall I?

Eat your tea please   →   Would you like to use your spoon or fork for that mouthful?

Make a list of any routine tasks that you are currently struggling with. Create and write down some effective choices to offer your child for when the situation arises next time. Remember to assume that they will do what you want them to do and make the choices appealing and appropriate for your child. Practise saying these words now, so that you are familiar and comfortable with how you will sound and feel when you use them for real.

And finally ...

Making choices, however small, is good for you! Offer choices to your children whenever you can. It's a great way to show your respect and make things a lot more fun!

You can choose to celebrate "No!" as a sign of growing independence in your child and use choices to help them develop this independence.

How this method worked for ...

Mel

Offering choices is a method I come back to again and again. It's so straightforward and effective when I remember to do it. My children know all about it too and often ask to be given a choice.

The other day, I offered my 3-year-old the choice of his red or blue trousers, assuming he would get dressed. He appeared to see through the choice and said, "I'm not getting dressed." My immediate reaction was that the choice hadn't worked but then I decided to just be really straight with him. I told him, "That's not the choice. We both need to get dressed. Your choice is what you wear."

He looked kind of disappointed for a moment and I began to think I'd need to try something else when he started rummaging in his drawer. He pulled out his brown dungarees and announced that he was going to wear them.
Result!

Chris

My 4-year-old has recently decided to be in charge by saying "No!" to me whenever she can, telling me that everything I do is wrong somehow and that everything must go her way! I have come to the conclusion that, from her point of view, she feels powerless (she is the youngest of three). I'm making a conscious effort to give her more choices (that also work for me!) so that she can feel more in charge of her life. For example, I'm letting her have friends to play more often and letting her choose which friends she wants to come round. This has the added benefit that we both get a break from each other!
Result!

Get a "Yes!"

Life is full of mundane, routine tasks. How enthusiastic can you get about washing, grocery shopping, cooking, tidying up …? One way to motivate yourself to do these things is to look beyond the task and focus on the benefits of the task being done. Then, instead of saying "No!" to doing the task, you're saying "Yes!" to the benefits. So:

• grocery shopping	*becomes*	having what you need to hand
• peeling veggies	*becomes*	sitting down to a tasty meal
• tidying up	*becomes*	finding things easily, living in a clear space
• going to work	*becomes*	having a holiday?!

and so on. Once you're focusing on these benefits, the task becomes easier and may even just kind of happen, without you really noticing! You can use this approach to motivate your children too.

The method

Think beyond the immediate task and ask yourself:

What will it get for my child? or **What's in it for them?**

Then simply ask them if they want this benefit. You know your children best: What's going to spark their interest and get them saying "Yes!"?

Here are two examples:

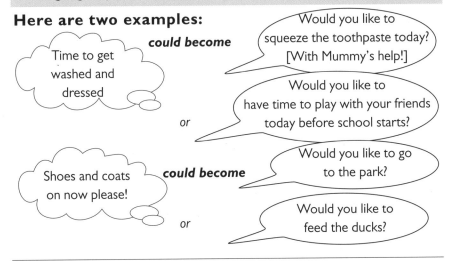

Section I

Tips for good results

✓ This approach works best when you get the "Yes" first, before mentioning anything about the task that needs to be done. This is because the "Yes" effectively bypasses any resistance they may have to the task. Things will then go more smoothly. Here's an example:

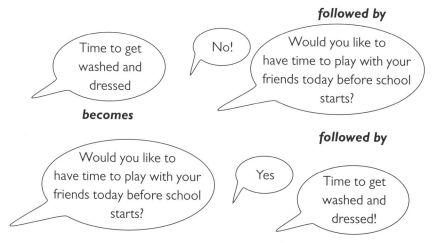

In the first scenario, the resistance created by the "No!" needs to be overcome. However, in the second scenario, they haven't expressed any resistance so there is less or none to overcome!

For a child who is very familiar with the task, the following scenario works even better because you don't even mention the task! It's also a nice way of showing respect for your child as you're showing them that you know you don't need to tell them exactly what to do.

✓ Once they're "hooked" on what's in it for them and have started the task, their attention may start to wander. You can keep them focused and speed them up by emphasising what's in it for them. Here are some examples:

Get a "Yes"　　　　　***E**mphasise what's in it for them*　　　　　***S**peed them up*

> Would you like to go to the park?

> What will you play on first at the park?

> Let's be quick so you can go to the park …

Get a "Yes"　　　　　***E**mphasise what's in it for them*　　　　　***S**peed them up*

> Would you like to squeeze your toothpaste today?

> How much toothpaste will you squeeze onto your brush?

> Let's be quick so you've got time to squeeze the toothpaste …

Get a "Yes"　　　　　***E**mphasise what's in it for them*　　　　　***S**peed them up*

> Would you like to have time to play with your friends today before school starts?

> Who would you like to play with before school starts?

> Let's be quick so there's time for you to play …

In the moment

Now you have a go

For the following tasks, ask yourself

What will it get for my child? or What's in it for them?

Cover up the suggestions on the right hand side until you have some suggestions of your own. Remember there's no right answer; your suggestion is probably more likely to work with your child, as you know them best.

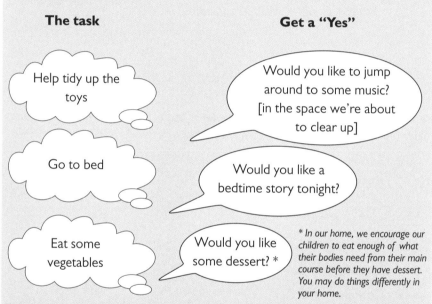

The task   **Get a "Yes"**

Help tidy up the toys

Would you like to jump around to some music? [in the space we're about to clear up]

Go to bed

Would you like a bedtime story tonight?

Eat some vegetables

Would you like some dessert? *

* In our home, we encourage our children to eat enough of what their bodies need from their main course before they have dessert. You may do things differently in your home.

If these are tasks you currently struggle with, think about and practise the words you have come up with, so that you're ready to use them for next time.

For any other routine tasks that you are currently struggling with, consider

What benefit does it get for your child? or What's in it for them?

In the same way, think about and practise saying the words you have come up with, so that you're ready to use them next time.

And finally ...

Children often know precisely what everyday tasks need to be done. Like you, they get on with tasks more quickly and easily if they're focusing on the benefits that the task will get for them. So next time you're about to say, "Come and ..." and you just know they're going to say "No!", think **Y-E-S**:

Y   Get a "**Y**es" by asking yourself: "What's in it for them?"
E   **E**mphasise what's in it for them to keep them focused on the task in hand
S   **S**peed them up by reminding them why they want to get finished in time.

You may be surprised by how much cooperation you get!

Does this sound like bribery? If this method is used to offer treats, sweets or another kind of short-term "pay off", then yes, it could be seen as bribery. A short-term treat holds no longer-term interest or gain for your child. When you use this method to offer your child benefits that are genuinely in their best interests in the long run – such as learning to squeeze toothpaste or getting to play with their friends – then it teaches useful motivational and negotiating skills.

How this method worked for ...

Helga

I used to find my weekly supermarket shop really stressful but now I get my son to focus on the benefits of getting the shopping finished with his help and cooperation: a go on the ride outside the supermarket entrance. I involve him in the shop as much as possible, getting him to choose the fruit and vegetables and asking him which cereal he would like that week. I can use his ride at the end of the shop as an incentive for good behaviour as necessary. It has changed the weekly shop from a stressful battle to actually enjoying spending time with my little boy.

I also use this method when he is occasionally clingy and reluctant to be dropped off at nursery. Instead of trying to stop him getting upset, I focus on what will happen when I collect him, e.g. I'll bring his bike and we can cycle home. This really helps to ease the situation.

Result!

In the moment

Rebecca

I found my 1-year-old and 2-year-old sons fighting over a toy car. My 2-year-old had seen his younger brother playing with his favourite car and wanted it back. Neither party would relinquish the toy, so I asked my eldest if he could find another car for his brother to play with and see if he could do a swap. He duly found another similar car and offered it to his brother, who was delighted with the deal. Peace was restored. I've seen him use this technique to successfully get a "Yes!" from his younger brother many times since.

Result!

Be impressed! Give praise the *EASY* way

5

☺ The porch in our house is where we keep all our coats and shoes. It also functions as an imaginary café, where the kids play with their pretend kitchen stuff. It's not a big space; you can imagine the chaos. One day, to my amazement, my 4-year-old spontaneously tidied up all the shoes! I was obviously delighted and wanted to acknowledge and encourage this behaviour.

☺ One weekend, we were having a lie in while our children played downstairs. When we came downstairs, we were amazed to discover that they had laid the table for breakfast and had already eaten!

☺ I am constantly delighted at how often my children *do* play nicely together and enjoy each other's company … all that time between scuffles! They really are nice kids and are developing their friendship.

Children are amazing and they do wonderful things! Giving effective praise is a great way to notice and acknowledge what you love about your children. It's also good parenting to notice and reinforce desirable behaviours and the qualities you want to encourage, such as independence, kindness, being helpful and so on. It makes a long term difference to your child's self-esteem, their sense of identity and their ability to give praise – to themselves and others.

The method

Here is a method for giving your child *effective* praise that:

- helps them know exactly what they've done that's great, so that they know what to do more of

- helps them identify their positive qualities and develop a positive sense of themselves.

In the moment

E What's the **Evidence?** Notice how your child's actions are producing something useful or a good result. Tell your child what you notice.

A What specific **Action** has your child taken? Notice what your child has done and how they have done it. Tell them this and clearly label their behaviour so they know what it is called.

S What does this **Say** or **Show** about **Your child?** Think about how your
Y child's actions demonstrate qualities that you want them to have, such as beng helpful or kind. Tell them how glad you are that they have or are developing these qualities.

Here are two examples:

You serve up a healthy meal for your family. Your child eats it quickly and easily. When they have finished, what do you say?

E   What's the *Evidence?*   You've eaten all your food!

A   What specific *Action* has your child taken?   You ate that really quickly and easily! Well done!

S
Y   What does this *Say or Show* about *Your child?*   You really enjoy eating good food! That's what your body needs. What a healthy boy you are!

Your children have been playing really well together, sharing building bricks to make a village. Now it's time for tea. What do you say?

E What's the *Evidence?*

What a brilliant village you've made!

A What specific *Action* has your child taken?

You're sharing the bricks and having a great game together.

S
Y

What does this *Say or Show* about *Your child?*

I'm really glad you get along so well.

Would you like to play some more after tea? [This follow up question uses **Get a "Yes!"**, page 45]

Tips for good results

✓ Be impressed! Show your enthusiasm for what your children do.

✓ Be sure to comment on the **E**vidence and **A**ction. Preferably do this before going on to say what this **S**ays or **S**hows about **Y**our child. This is because your child can directly experience and observe the **E**vidence and **A**ction so they are more likely to understand what you are talking about. For example:

"Good boy! Well done!"

gives no indication of what your child has done that you think is *good*.

In the moment

Whereas,

"What a lovely tidy space!" (**E**vidence)

"You've done a great job of putting your toys away." (**A**ction)

explains what you are impressed with. When you follow this up with

"Good boy! Well done!" (What this **S**ays about **Y**our child)

you are now being clear about what you mean by *good*.

✓ Be specific in your choice and use of words so that your child understands and associates these words with their behaviour and themselves, e.g. quick, easy, organised, helpful, tidy, careful, calm, smart, caring, healthy, strong, polite, clever. You choose: what qualities are important to you?

✓ Avoid the "sting in the tail" that so effectively negates praise, comments such as:

- "You've eaten all your dinner *for once!*"
- "You've eaten really fast. *Eat more slowly next time.*"
- "You're helping tidy up. *Wonders will never cease …*"

You know the kind of thing!

✓ Traditionally, praise is given for something you've done. But with young children, you can use praise in anticipation of desirable behaviour to actively encourage and persuade them to do it. For example, saying "Good boy" in an impressed tone of voice as you offer your child some clothes encourages him to take the clothes and try to put them on. Mary explains how this tip worked for her at the end of this section (page 57).

✓ Make a real effort to notice your child doing useful, appropriate things, however small or slow! It's all too easy to ignore their efforts and dive in and take over instead. Give them as much time as they need, so that they can make progress. Then you and they can *be impressed!* Now, you may think that you don't have time for this, especially if you're up against the clock. However, if you can stay calm and open to their efforts, it can often work out quicker and easier for all concerned.

✓ Treasure the compliments about your children that other people give you. Accept them with thanks as a true reflection of how others see your children. Pass them on to your children as appropriate.

✓ Use this method more generally for giving effective compliments and thanks to others.

✓ Explore how to celebrate your own successes, how to **Be impressed ... with *You!*** (page 153).

Now you have a go

Think of situations where your child's behaviour really impresses you.

E What's the **Evidence** for their impressive behaviour? What have they achieved?

A What specific **Action** has your child taken? What have they done and how have they done it?

S What does this **Say** or **Show** about **Your child?** What qualities is your child

Y demonstrating that you want to highlight and encourage?

If you wish, write down and practise what you want to say so that next time you notice this behaviour, you can be impressed!

Write down the words you currently and habitually use to praise your child. Do they incorporate the principles of the **EASY** method to name and highlight the behaviour and the qualities you want to acknowledge and reinforce in your child? Modify and expand them as necessary to incorporate these principles.

When you think of your parents and the things they used to say to you, what phrases or sayings come to mind? What would you like your children to remember you saying to them? Write these phrases down and make sure you say them frequently. You could even make them your catch phrases!

In the moment

And finally...

As a parent, your attention is inevitably drawn to any undesirable or potentially dangerous behaviour from your children. This is because you may need to intervene to ensure their safety and welfare and perhaps the welfare of others too. This method gives you a concrete way to notice desirable behaviour from your children by giving them effective praise whenever you can. Draw attention to the many wonderful things your children do. Build their self-esteem and balance out and exceed the critical feedback that is an inevitable part of life.

Let your children hear you saying the kinds of things you want them to say to others and to themselves. You know you're doing a good job when you hear your children praising each other.

Wow Joe, that's brilliant! You've drawn a lovely smiley face!

Thank you for letting me open one of your birthday presents Hannah. You're really kind.

How this method worked for...

Shirley

*In the morning, I laid out my son's clothes and encouraged him to get dressed while I had a shower. When I got out he had put his pants on. I could have been frustrated at the fact that he hadn't put all his clothes on, but I decided to **be impressed** at what he had done: I said, "Look at you! You've got your pants on! You're doing a great job of getting dressed! You're such a big boy getting dressed all by yourself!" And, to my delight, he carried on getting dressed as I did too!*

Result!

Mary

Not long after my first child learned to walk, I really enjoyed taking her to parks and play areas, delighted to watch her toddling around, exploring and developing her balance and coordination. Trouble was, when it came to the play areas, she was more interested in other people's buggies than in the play equipment. At nursery too, her interest in buggies was becoming rather a nuisance as she wanted to push, rock and play with the ones that held babies having their naps! One afternoon, when I went to pick her up, I observed her doing this as she was more interested in a buggy than my arrival!

I managed to turn my urge to say, "Don't play with the buggy!" into "Hey, come and look at this book ..." as I chose an animal board book and acted really interested in it. This caught her attention enough to cause her to stop and turn round to me but even as I encouraged her to look at the book saying, "Look at this ... What's this animal?" she was starting to turn back to the buggy ... "Good girl, let's read together" I said on impulse, acting as if she was coming over to me to read the book ... and to my surprise and delight, she did turn and come to me! Giving her a taste of the praise she would get for coming to me seemed to tip the balance.

Result!

Get down to their level

Take a look at the following pictures. Which pictures do you think show easy, comfortable conversations? How do you know?

And these?

Engaging with someone else, connecting with them to get your message across, is much more likely to happen if you're **on a level** with them because:

- It's easier to make eye contact and hear each other.

- The equality of height implies that both of you have equal worth in the conversation.

- It's harder to ignore the other person because their face is right there in front of you!

on a level

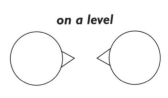

Conversely, being at different physical levels makes it harder for you to connect and engage with someone because:

- It's harder to make eye contact or hear each other.

- The difference in heights can imply an inequality of power. Being higher up may mean you have some kind of power and control over others. Over time, they may come to resent this. As a parent, you do have power so it's important you use it wisely and fairly – see **Set and maintain reasonable boundaries** (page 89).

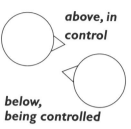

above, in control

below, being controlled

- Being at the lower level, it's easier to get distracted because you have to keep looking up and concentrating on what the other person is saying.

Parents are obviously bigger than their children so they spend a lot of time above them. There's this kind of *adult world* above the *children's world* where you can have (or briefly snatch!) adult conversations, exchange remarks, jokes and stories, literally talking over the heads of your children. No wonder then, when you speak to your children from the *adult world*, they pay little attention to you and it's easy for them to disregard what you say.

So when you want to engage with your children, it's a good idea to **get down to their level**. By doing this you are demonstrating your willingness to enter *their world* so that you can better understand what's going on for them.

The method

Whenever your child appears to be ignoring you, your message doesn't seem to be getting through or you don't understand what your child is trying to communicate, move and change your position as necessary to get down to their level.

Here's an example:

Your child is eating at the kitchen table while you are making yourself a drink. You notice them playing with their food instead of eating it. From across the kitchen, you politely say, "Eat your food properly with your spoon please." Your child appears to ignore you completely. You move closer and try again. No response. You are now standing over them about to get cross when you notice that your child is totally absorbed in what they are doing. They are oblivious to you. ***Getting down to their level*** surprises them; you notice for the first time what fun they are having. Now you are in a position to explain that their food is for eating with a spoon and you then help them to do it.

Tips for good results

✓ When your child wants you to pick them up, you can interpret this as their way of trying to get onto the same level with you. You then have a choice: you can bring them up to your level or you can get down to their level. As your child gets bigger and heavier, getting down to their level can be more physically comfortable. It also opens up more possibilities for ways forward because you can see what's happening for them at their level. Picking them up also eventually leads to having to put them down again! Nicky explains how this worked for her at the end of this section (page 62).

✓ Sitting on a low stool or chair as your child stands beside you is another way to be at their level. It can offer some relief from sitting on the floor and is also a great way to have a cuddle!

Now you have a go

Think about what it's like to have someone towering over you. Ideally, get another adult to stand on a chair and look down at you. Have a chat with your friend up there. How does that feel for you? This is what our children experience most of the time.

Now have your friend on the chair put their hands on their hips and look down at you sternly and crossly... Scary isn't it?! As your friend gets off the chair and comes back down to your level, notice how the feeling between you changes.

Remember how a difference in height affects the conversation and your relationship.

And finally ...

Getting down on a level with your children is so simple but also very powerful. Like turning Don'ts into Do's, and Stop's into Go's, it's a method that you can apply again and again, to great effect.

Being on a level with someone is key to communicating respectfully with them. We know this is the case with adults so let's show our children the same respect.

How this method worked for ...

Sharon

I was dropping my son off at nursery. I was stood up, catching brief snatches of conversation with the staff and other parents whilst also trying to say goodbye to my son. He started to make a fuss, clinging on to my leg, which really surprised and confused me because he was usually fine when I left him. It became a bit of a fight with me trying to get him off me until I eventually moved and got down to his level. On a level with him, he told me he just wanted to "say goodbye properly!" We had a kiss and a hug and off he went to play!

Result!

Nicky

I used to get very frustrated with my daughter when we went for a walk because she always seemed to "want a carry". One day, instead of getting frustrated, I got down to her level. I immediately got a sense of how dull it was for her so I stayed down and we looked around and found some interesting leaves. She was then quite happy to walk on and we continued to find things at her level to keep her interested.

I feel less annoyed now when I do carry her for a bit because I think of it as us being on a level together, instead of her being lazy.

Result!

Kathryn

Once all my kids were at school and I went to pick them up in the afternoon, my youngest would be really difficult, pulling on my leg, sitting on the floor and generally refusing to walk home. When I simply got down to her level and asked what was up, she told me how tired she was and that she didn't want to walk home. From this position, I was able to acknowledge her and her tiredness. I was then able to **Get a "Yes!"** *(page 45) more easily and keep her focused on all the things she wanted to do when we got back at home.*

Result!

Move beside

One morning, my 3-year-old was kneeling on the floor engrossed in drawing a picture. As I walked past, I stopped, looked down and commented on what a lovely picture she was drawing. She looked up at me with a scowl and said, "Now you've spoilt it, Mummy!"

My perhaps rather superficial encouragement had clearly not been well received! As I looked down at her, I realised that a part of me was hooked by her annoyance and I wanted to respond in a confrontational manner by saying something along the lines of, "All right, calm down, I was only trying to be encouraging!" However, I realised that she was only 3 and I had clearly annoyed her, so a better idea was to "make things right" in whatever way I could.

I couldn't think of anything useful to say and knew that if I just walked away, this would provoke her. So I simply dropped down to her level. I then had a sense of her wanting me to "get out of her face", so I moved to be beside and slightly behind her. From this position I could now see and feel for myself how distracting and interfering my interruption could have seemed to her. Still without saying anything, I acknowledged this to myself and felt warmth and sympathy for her. After a few moments of being together like this, I noticed that her attention had returned to her picture, so I simply "melted away", backing off and moving away to carry on with what I had been doing. A little while later she came and showed me her picture. **Result!**

How you position yourself when you engage with someone sends out a very clear non-verbal message to them. We explored the impact of height in the previous **Get down to their level** method, so now let's consider the impact of orientation:

face-to-face

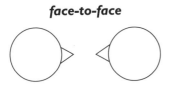

Being *face-to-face* with someone can be associated with either confrontation or intimacy. These are two extremes of connection between two people. Being face-to-face can feel very direct, with a sense of total commitment and "no way out".

In the moment

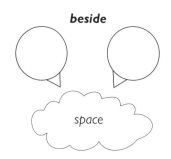

beside

space

Being *beside* someone is associated with being united with them as equals in some way. This could be united against a common threat, united in seeking a solution to a shared problem or simply united in easy company. This connection is less direct and intense than being face-to-face, with a sense of movement and flexibility. There is also a sense of the space in front of you being available or "open" for you to both consider something in partnership.

Our children challenge us and, before we know it, we can sometimes find ourselves in a face-to-face confrontation. The following method is great for defusing these situations.

The method

Whenever you find yourself in a face-to-face confrontation with your child, recognise that it only takes the slightest movement for you to change your orientation from this face-to-face "stand-off" and to **move beside**.

From your current face-to-face position, break eye contact, look away slightly to one side and allow your body to follow with a slight turn to that side:

from

to

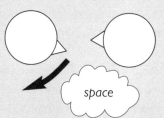

space

Notice how, although this turning movement is very small, it has the effect of turning your attention to the space that opens up in front of you both.

Now wait. Allow a few moments of calm as you both adjust to how your connection has changed. In these moments, it helps to focus on that shared space opening up in front of you, and how you and your child can sort things out in this space.

Tune in to your child's response and, as you feel calmer, go with whatever approach now seems appropriate.

Here's an example:

Your children are playing outside with some mud. You tell them not to bring the mud into the house and to just play with it outside. A while later, you are annoyed to find a trail of mud up to the bathroom where there is a muddy bucket on the floor. One of your children is running water at the sink. As you exclaim, "What a mess!" your child faces up to you, defiant that they have come in to wash their bucket.

As you feel your anger rising and sense a "stand-off" with your child, you **look away slightly to one side and allow your body to follow with a slight turn to that side**. In the space this opens up, you can see the muddy bucket on the floor and your anger is now directed at that.

Now wait. Allow a few moments of calm as you both adjust to how your connection has changed. From being angry at your child, your focus has changed to being angry at all the mud. You are now in a position to explain to your child that you are cross about all the mud in the house and that this is why we play with mud outside.

Tune in to your child's response and, as you feel calmer, go with whatever approach now seems appropriate. Your child assures you that they will clean it up. You know they will make an even bigger mess of the floor, so you ask them to clean up themselves and the sink while you clean the floor.

Instead of spending your time getting really cross with your child, you're now cleaning up the mess together. You make a mental note to give them a bowl of water outside next time they want to play with mud. Then they can wash up outside too.

Tips for good results

In the moment

✓ The movements need to be small so that you maintain your connection with your child. Too big a movement will break your connection and can appear provocative. Sometimes, this will happen or indeed you may intentionally break your connection so that you can take responsibility for yourself and manage your own needs. You perhaps recognise you need a **pause for thought** (page 139). In this case, be mindful of the impact that your "disconnect" may have had when you later re-connect with your child.

✓ Sometimes **moving beside** may feel like backing down. If you're honest, you want a confrontation! Accept that this is perhaps the best you can do in the circumstances but recognise you always have an option to **move beside**... Just trying it out can achieve some surprising results. See how this method worked for John, at the end of this section (page 67).

Now you have a go

With this method, you need to practise "the turn", i.e. **break eye contact, look away slightly to one side** and allow your body to follow with a slight turn to that side.

Practise turning your head slightly, your shoulders a touch, your hips just a fraction. The more you familiarise yourself with this movement, the more likely you are to try it out when you notice an opportunity. It can get to feel like a subtle dance step! Enjoy the physical and mental flexibility that this movement gives you in potentially highly charged situations.

And finally ...

Face-to-face confrontations often become **win-lose** situations: they end up with winners and losers. This kind of interaction can leave hurt and resentment that may resurface at a later date. **Moving beside** instantly breaks the dynamic of the confrontation and creates the potential for you to unite with your child to move forward together. Then you can both be winners in a **win-win** situation.

How this method worked for ...

Claire

My daughter wouldn't get undressed and wouldn't let me help her. It was bedtime and she was being really provocative, telling me to go away and so on. I thought I'd done a great job of staying calm, getting her up to the bathroom but now she was really winding me up. She was sat on the floor with her arms folded, glaring up at me. I was just about to threaten her with the worst possible negative consequences I could think of when I remembered to try "the turn". I broke eye contact and that slightest of movements allowed me to "unlock" myself from our stand-off.

It felt like backing down but I moved to sit down beside her on the floor. What a relief! I felt much calmer and I noticed her turning slightly to see what I was doing. So I nudged her very gently. She whined but I could feel us both calming down as I just sat there beside her... and she started to take off her socks! I continued to just sit there, not saying anything and she continued to get undressed and ready for bed at her own pace.
Result!

John

We were all tired and it was time to tidy up. For once, my youngest was getting on with it but my eldest was demanding that I help. I said I'd come and help when he'd made a start. He mimicked me back, saying that I should start first. I was surprised and annoyed by his rudeness and found myself squaring up to him to tell him off. I then remembered "the turn" – which is very similar to a karate avoidance technique I learned years ago – so I turned and looked away to the side, kind of brushing past him. This must have confused and perhaps amused him because he moved to pop up again right in front of me. So I turned again; he moved again. I turned, he moved. We ended up having a playful brawl for a couple of minutes which seemed to "fix" us because we then just got on and tidied up together!
Result!

Join them in their activity

2

Picture this:

You're busy doing something while someone else is talking to you. Maybe you're preparing a meal or looking for something while your partner or a friend is telling you something. You're kind of listening to them and make appropriate noises such as "Yes", "Aha", "I see ..." but actually, you're concentrating on what you're doing and haven't heard a word they've said.

Now imagine being on the other side of this experience:

Your friend or partner is busy doing something and you have something important to tell them. As you are speaking, you pick up that they're not actually paying any attention to you; they're totally absorbed in what they're doing. You stop talking. After a few minutes, if they are cooking a meal, you might ask, "What can I do to help?" Or, if they're looking for something, you might ask, "What are you looking for?" as you start to help them look.

As soon as you **join them in their activity**, they may well stop and say something like, "Oh, thanks ... What were you saying?" Once you have this level of engagement and connection with each other, you can work together and have a proper conversation.

It's just the same for children, only more so! It's really hard for them to break off from what they're doing because they get so absorbed, taking so much in and learning fast. They need to be focused and determined because there is so much to learn.

Just like with your adult friends, your children are not intentionally ignoring you. They are simply busy elsewhere. As with adults, a respectful way to make your presence known so that you can connect with your children is to **join them in their activity**.

The method

Notice

Notice what your children are doing.

Think outcome and time

Decide what outcome you want: do you need to move your children on or do you simply want to spend some time with them? How much time have you got?

Level and beside

Approach them calmly, get down to their level and position yourself to be beside them (as explored in the previous two methods **Get down to their level** and **Move beside**).

Take an interest

Take an interest in what they're doing: look, listen and "tune in". When you feel you have a real sense of what's going on, comment on what you see, hear and feel.

Wait to connect

Wait until you get some kind of response from your children – verbal or non-verbal – to your comment. Make another comment if necessary. When you get a response, you know you have a connection.

Moving on

You can now get more involved in their activity as much or as little as feels right and time allows. The more involved you are, the more opportunities you will find to incorporate their activity into moving them on, if this is what you need to do.

Here's an example:

Notice

The children are playing "Catching the train" under the stairs.

Think outcome and time

*The **outcome** I need is to get them upstairs to wash and dress in **20 minutes**, ready to take them on to nursery and school.*

Level and beside

I'm crouching down beside my youngest.

Take an interest

My youngest is using dominoes as tickets whilst my eldest is putting teddies on the children's seats they've arranged to make their "train". I ask: "Where are you going today?"

Wait to connect

My eldest says, "York", where we went last weekend.

Moving on

I tell them I'd like to catch the train to the bathroom so my youngest gives me a "ticket" – a domino. I really know I'm in now! I encourage them to take me to the bathroom on their "train". My eldest leads the way and my youngest takes the dominoes to give out more "tickets". Each task (e.g. pyjamas off, wash face, clean teeth, etc.) becomes a "station" and each child gets another "ticket" when they've completed the task. We're all happy to continue the imaginary train game. They're ready in half the time it can often take!

Tips for good results

✓ This method is obviously a great way for you to develop your relationships with your children: to find out about what they currently enjoy and to have lively, imaginative conversations and negotiations with them.

✓ As you **join them in their activity**, be sensitive to the responses of your children. You will know if your approach is unwelcome in which case, if time allows, back off and leave them be. However, if you need to move them on, wait and allow them to adjust to your presence. Be as gentle and patient as you can to give them the chance to decide to move on. Accept that sometimes you will just have to "call time".

✓ Be prepared to negotiate about how you and your children will move on. Allow them to do things their way as much as possible: it makes it more likely that they will do it. It's also well worth letting them have the last word so they feel that they have taken the initiative and decided to move on.

✓ Make sure that you are ready to notice your children and what they are doing if you want to use this method. If you're in a bad mood and need some attention yourself, the methods in Section 3 (**Take care of YOU**, page 135) will serve you well. You will know when you're ready to come back to this method.

✓ Sometimes, you may not think you have enough time, energy or imagination to **join them in their activity**. That's OK as that's life sometimes. Accept this is where you're at. However, bear in mind that:

- children often do things more quickly if they want to and think that they decided to (just like adults!).
- you don't actually need much imagination; your children have loads of it. Be impressed! All you need to do is let them continue to use their imagination in what you now need them to do.
- you may have more time, energy or imagination than you realised ...

✓ As your children get older, when you have joined them in their activity and connected with them, you can simply ask them how they would like to do what needs to be done.

Now you have a go

You are undoubtedly joining others in their activities already, whether you are aware of it or not. It is a natural part of being curious about and relating to other human beings. Think back and recall happy times you have spent with others, especially your children. Notice how these times either involved you joining them in their activity or vice versa. The activities then became enjoyable, shared experiences.

Now you have increased your awareness of how you already join others in their activities, you can use this method to do it more and especially with your children. Do it as much as you can, whenever you can. It's a particularly useful approach for simply **spending more time** with your children and for **easing flashpoints** in your day.

Spending more time

Think of opportunities when you would like to spend time with your children. The next time an opportunity arises, be ready to join them in their activity. Be prepared to notice and go along with what they are doing or want to do as much as possible. Be sure to join them in *their* activity.

Easing flashpoints

Consider what your children are engrossed in doing when flashpoints occur in your day. Imagine what it would be like to join them in these activities and how you might incorporate or develop them towards what you need to happen. You are now ready to try this out next time the situation occurs.

Alternatively, while you are considering these flashpoints, you may realise that you're better off using a different method to direct your children towards more useful activities at these times. That's equally useful learning. Well done!

And finally ...

Joining your child in their activity, in *their world*, is a great way to develop your relationship. It can also be the source of a great deal of pleasure, fun and love in family life. While keeping one foot in the adult world, it's also an opportunity for you to rediscover your own imagination and creativity: the "inner child" that's still alive and kicking in you!

How this method worked for ...

Maria

I realised I hadn't actually spent much one-to-one time with my youngest and even felt like I was missing her! So next time I got the chance, I joined her in her activity. She was well into this imaginary game where she was the teacher. As I watched and listened, she quickly included me in as her assistant. We had a lovely time, setting lots of "hard work" for all her "class". I really enjoyed visiting her in her world.

Result!

Mark

I was looking after my daughter one rainy afternoon and she was really busy in her play café, making meals for her toys to have a pretend picnic. We were having sandwiches for tea, so I asked her if she wanted to join the toys and have a real, indoor picnic. We had a great time. I really enjoyed being able to incorporate her game into what we needed to do anyway.

Result!

Carol

I was getting fed up with all my family because their standard response to any and every request I made seemed to be "Just a minute ..." So the next time I heard it — which was from my eldest — instead of getting cross, I decided to go and join her in her activity. It turned out she was colouring in and just wanted to finish the bit she was doing. Fair enough. Then, with my youngest, he was playing with his toy cars and just wanted to park them all up properly. Fair enough. My partner was just finishing putting some dry clothes away. Thank you! And so on ... I've done this enough now to realise that "Just a minute ..." is nothing personal and I say it myself!

Result!

Putting it all together

The previous three methods have all explored becoming more aware of how you use your body, your physical self, to make a good connection with your children. However well chosen your words may be, they're unlikely to get through to your children unless you first make a good connection with them. It's like making a phone call: you need to make sure the person you're calling is at the other end before you can have a conversation!

There are other aspects of your physical presence that can also have a major impact on the connection you make with your child. These include your:

- eye contact
- voice quality, tone and volume
- facial expression
- sensitivity to personal space.

Notice how you use these and the impact they have on situations. They will further increase your flexibility and your ability to communicate effectively and respectfully with your children.

Matching and mismatching

Making a good connection with your child is all about trying to **match** their physical presence as much as possible. Doing this sincerely gives your child a very strong non-verbal message of respect and love for them and *their world*. It's great to practise **matching** with your children; it shows them the same respect you would show to anyone else. It's also great because you can be more purposeful, obvious and playful with children; with adults it usually requires a bit more subtlety!

There may be times when you're feeling stressed, cross or perhaps about to "lose it". **Mismatching** can be a useful technique at these times. As the name suggests, it involves doing the opposite to **matching**, to effectively disconnect yourself from your child. For example, standing up and moving away from your child minimises the impact of your emotions on them and creates an opportunity (however brief!) for you to calm down and find a better way forward. See **pause for thought** (page 139) for more ways to give yourself a moment to gather yourself and acknowledge your needs before looking for more positive ways forward.

In the moment

The power of a *consistent* demonstration "Do as I say *and* as I do"

Putting these methods of *non-verbal* communication together with the methods on *verbal* communication, you have the ingredients for clear and consistent communication with your children that is both positive and respectful. One of the tips for good results in the **Turn Don'ts into Do's** method has already suggested the power of using a demonstration that is consistent with your words. For example, "We eat yoghurt like this …" with a clear demonstration as you spoon your yoghurt into your mouth.

It's helpful to be consistent in what you say and do. However, inconsistencies between verbal and non-verbal communication can and do happen. For example:

Speak nicely to me!   said in an authoritative and harsh tone

Here, let me help you …   said in an impatient and unhelpful tone

I'm waiting for you …   as you remember something and go to get it

I am not tired!   whilst having a big yawn!

Being aware of these kinds of inconsistency gives you the opportunity to notice and correct them whenever you can, by adjusting your voice tone, your body language or your actions. By making these adjustments, you are giving your children clearer and more consistent messages. It can also minimise being on the receiving end of inconsistent messages from your children, as what you do your children will surely copy! (**It's cool to copy!** page 193, has more on this.)

And finally …

All the methods in this section encourage you to *notice* your children: to tune in, look, listen and warm to them and whatever they're involved in. Paying close attention to your children enables you to appreciate just how amazing they are. Being impressed and inspired by them will lead you to show genuine respect for them and *their world*.

How putting it all together worked for ...

Dawn

For several mornings in a row, I had ended up shouting at my children to come and sit up for breakfast like an army sergeant major. They were playing in a room adjacent to the kitchen and, in spite of being able to hear me perfectly well, they wouldn't respond to my initially polite requests for them to come for breakfast. The next morning, I was about to start shouting again when I realised that my message wasn't getting through.

*In that same moment, I recalled how, before we had children, my partner would sit on the floor reading the Sunday paper in the exact same spot as the kids were playing. He would get very absorbed in what he was reading. If I wanted him to do something, I would go and **get down to his level**, sitting with him on the floor. I would then **join him in his activity** by asking him what he was reading. He would then show me what he was reading so I would **move beside** him to look. From there on, we would talk easily with each other and I would get a fair and reasonable response to my request for his help. I don't ever recall shouting at him like I was shouting at our children.*

I felt ashamed of myself as I realised how disrespectful I had been in the way I had been "communicating" with our children. So I simply went over to them, got down to their level and noticed that they were colouring. I asked them to finish the bit they were colouring and then come to the table ... which they did without any fuss or bother.
Result!

Heather

I'd taken my 2-year-old to the doctors for morning surgery. She had a mild rash that I wanted checking out although it wasn't bothering her at all. The doctor was running late and we were last so we came out into the empty surgery car park at nearly 12.30 p.m. We were both fed up and very hungry by this point so I just wanted to get home as soon as possible to get lunch. I opened the car door for my daughter to climb in but my heart sank as she turned her back on me and started to sing the "Hokey Cokey", wiggling around in the middle of the car park.

*I wasn't feeling at all "resourceful" and was resigning myself to having to manhandle her into the car when I thought I might as well try some of this **Happy Kids Happy***

You stuff. There was no way I was going to **get down to her level** or **join her in her activity** – I just didn't have the patience for it. I thought about **offering choices** but knew, "Would you like to clip yourself into your car seat or shall I?" would fall on deaf ears.

As a last ditch, half-hearted attempt, I decided to try to **get a "Yes!"** and asked her, "Would you like to listen to some music on the way home?" To my amazement, she stopped dancing. She slowly turned round. She slowly walked up to the car and climbed in. She clipped herself in and said, "Mummy, I want 'Wind the Bobbin Up' please".
Result!

Section 2

More challenging situations

Thinking differently

opens up new ways forward

Introduction

The methods in Section 1 gave you quick ways to **say** and **do** something useful *in the moment*; ways of dealing with everyday niggles and for keeping things running smoothly. Sometimes, though, your child's behaviour and the situations you're in challenge you. Despite your best efforts to say and do something useful, you're not happy with how you're dealing with a situation as a parent and you're not getting the results you want.

The methods in this section involve taking time out to explore a situation from a different perspective. This enables you to gain new information: to **think** differently, unravel challenging behaviour and gain new insights into what makes your child tick. You are then equipped to find new ways forward that are better for all concerned.

The mirror symbol beside these methods indicates that you'll need a little calm time out to reflect on what's going on. Exploring challenging situations and behaviours in this way will make a significant, positive difference to how you think about and relate to your child. And, with a little practice, you'll also be able to use these methods *in the moment*.

The first three methods give you ways to prepare the ground and get clearer about what you want in your family life. You'll then be able to create and sustain an environment that nurtures positive behaviour and healthy, happy relationships.

The methods are:

- What you focus on is what you get
- Set and maintain reasonable boundaries
- Give and take: the *dance* of responsibility.

Then there are three methods to help you find new, more effective ways of dealing with those situations and behaviours that catch you out or are really getting to you. Your current response ranges from feeling perplexed and confused, where you just *don't get* what your child's behaviour is all about, right through to feeling personally challenged, exasperated and "losing it".

The methods are:

- Find a useful meaning
- Clean up your thinking
- Find out what your body knows.

What you focus on is what you get

Have you noticed that …

When you were pregnant, or when you were thinking about having children, suddenly the world was full of pregnant women?

or

When you needed to get a buggy or pram, suddenly they were everywhere. They were always passing you … or you were always tripping over them! And you became particularly aware of that particular model (and colour) that you *really* wanted?

Isn't it interesting that **what you're thinking about and what you're focusing on is what you notice and what you get more of?**

😞 So if you're thinking about what you *don't* want, if you have a really clear picture and expectation of what you *don't* want to happen, *that's* what you'll get more of.

🙂 On the other hand, if you practise thinking about what you *do* want, if you have a really clear picture and expectation of what you *do* want to happen, *that's* what you'll get more of.

By focusing on what you want for yourself, your children and your whole family, you are choosing to get more of those things. So it's worth developing your ability to identify what you want and then maintaining your focus on it.

The method

Here are two ways of developing your ability to focus on what you want for yourself, your children and your family life.

For yourself: Whenever you catch yourself thinking about what you don't want, ask yourself

What do I want *instead?*

and use positive language to answer this question.

This method is similar to **Turn Don'ts into Do's** (page 27), which uses positive language to change your child's behaviour. Now you are using positive language to change the way you're thinking.

Here are some examples:

I don't want

to miss the bus
to forget my appointment
to get angry

I do want

to catch the bus
to remember my appointment
to stay calm

This is a really simple way of noticing how you talk to yourself, your "self-talk", and making it more helpful and kind to you. (The **Give yourself a *good* talking to** method, page 163, has more on making your self-talk useful.)

For yourself, your children and your family life: Take time out to think about what you do want. This is particularly useful when you are concerned about a situation or a child's behaviour that you don't want. Ask yourself:

What do I want *instead?*

Imagine this in detail and anticipate what it will be like for you, your child and the rest of your family. Ask yourself:

- **How will this work?**
- **What will this look, sound and feel like?**
- **What will the benefits be for me, my child and my family?**

Here's an example:

 I **don't** want all this mess! I feel like I'm spending my life tidying up after my kids ... so that they can make more mess!

What do I want *instead*?

 This is a tricky question. I want ... a new house ... a month off in the Bahamas alone! Actually, I guess what I really want is for the kids to learn to tidy up after themselves. I want them to put their toys away when they have finished playing with them.

When I fully imagine and anticipate what this will be like for me, my children and our family life...

How will this work? What will this look, sound and feel like?

I need to consistently encourage and help them to tidy up so that it becomes routine ... fun even! Oh help! I need to keep my own things tidy too!

What will the benefits be for me, my child and my family?

This will teach us all to look after our things better. And maybe we'll get rid of stuff we don't use any more. We will enjoy having a clear, tidy space in which to play with the next toy or game ...

Tips for good results

✓ Check out the **Be impressed** method (page 51) for ways to notice, reinforce and encourage the behaviours you do want from your children.

✓ Children are natural mimics, so remember that if you want your child to do something, it helps if you do it too. This may challenge you to change your behaviour (**Walk your talk**, page 185, can help you do this).

✓ Thinking positively about what you want is easier if you're in a good mood. If your mood is less than good and trying to think positively is beginning to do your head in, then you will find that the methods in Section 3, **Take care of YOU** (page 135), will serve you well. Return to this method when you're ready.

More challenging situations

Now you have a go

For some more practice at turning your internal **don'ts** into **do's**, cover up the suggested **do's** below until you've come up with your own **do's**.

I don't want

to be lonely
to be tired
to shout

I do want

to be with my friends
to have lots of energy
to use my normal voice

Consider a situation or a behaviour that you **don't** want. Work through the questions:

What do I want *instead?*

When I fully imagine and anticipate what this will be like for me, my child and our family life...

- **How will this work?**
- **What will this look, sound and feel like?**
- **What will the benefits be for me, my child and my family?**

Have you now got some ideas for actions that will move you towards what you want? Check: are these things you can and will do? If so, decide when and how you will put them into practice. If not, ask yourself the questions again and this time focus on how what you want can work for you, your child and for your whole family – what the benefits will be.

And finally ...

Does all this sound like wearing rose-coloured glasses? Do you feel like you are just fooling yourself, denying all the bad stuff that does happen?

This method isn't about denying that difficult, challenging situations occur or that bad stuff does happen. This method is about recognising that you can choose what you focus on. You can focus on what you don't want and get more of that or you can focus on what you really want *as much as possible* and add to that!

It's your choice. So which do you choose?

How this method worked for ...

Alan

My middle child has various dietary allergies which means he often can't have what the rest of the family is eating and has to have a bland alternative. Mealtimes can become a battleground, trying to get him to eat anything and dealing with his complaints about it not being fair.

When I thought about what I wanted instead, I could picture us all sat around the table eating together. There was a hum of amicable chat along with some banter and laughter. As I really imagined and anticipated what this would be like, I realised that somehow we had to make it "fairer" for our middle son. As I stayed with my picture of harmony around the meal table, it occurred to me that, perhaps once or twice a week, we could all eat the same as him. The more I thought about this, the more it made sense as a way of integrating the family and helping us understand and support all our needs.
Result!

Karen

I have two boys aged 3 and 5. Although I was delighted they were both out of nappies and independent in their toileting, I was getting increasingly annoyed with the state of the bathroom. I would find a messy, unflushed toilet often with the tap left running and the towel and even the soap on the floor.

What I wanted instead was to walk into the bathroom and not know they'd been there: toilet clean and flushed, towel on the rail and taps off. When I thought about how this could work, I realised I needed to give them more positive direction and reinforcement of the behaviour I wanted. So I thought about and wrote down the steps for using the toilet including the order we do them in. I then clearly and calmly explained the steps to the boys.

For the next few days, I made sure I was on hand to remind them of the steps when they used the toilet. I also made sure I demonstrated and reinforced the steps whenever I used the toilet and they were with me. Finally, I wanted them to feel good about their toileting skills and to notice having a nice clean and tidy bathroom. So, whenever they've been to the toilet now, they come and ask me to check the bathroom. I give my eldest a tick on his chart and my youngest gets a sticker when they've completed the steps successfully. If they've missed anything, I ask them to check and finish off the steps before I give them their tick or sticker.

I'm amazed at the difference being positive and clear about the behaviour I want has made – a much nicer bathroom and two proud, happy boys.
Result!

More challenging situations

More challenging situations

Set and maintain reasonable boundaries

When I became a parent, I knew I was taking on many roles including carer, cook, nurse and chauffeur. It only dawned on me gradually, as my children started to challenge boundaries, that parenting also includes setting and maintaining boundaries.

Boundaries, limits and rules are important in creating an environment in which we can get along and live together. Boundaries give children the space to grow, learn and play; to develop an awareness of their relationships with others and what's important in life. Children need to challenge boundaries to feel secure within them and to be more creative within the limits they impose.

So as one of the "responsible adults" in our house, I knew I had to enforce boundaries but I didn't want to become a police officer.

Have you noticed that, when it comes to enforcing boundaries, we live in a **don't** world?

So we know really well what we *shouldn't* be doing! Expressing boundaries in this way gives us the limit beyond which we must not go. But what can we do instead? And if we did that, how would it look, sound and feel? As we already know from the **Turn Don'ts into Do's** method (page 27) it's much more effective to tell children what we do want them to do.

Here are three possible ways to enforce boundaries:

Turn Don'ts into Do's method (page 27)

I **win**
You **lose**   I have the power and you are weak. I maintain boundaries by enforcing compliance. I use **don't** a lot because I am focusing on stopping you crossing the boundary (which you try to do a lot).
You will do as I say.

I **lose**
You **win**   You are strong and I am weak. I try to enforce the boundaries but give in when you resist. I abdicate my responsibility for enforcing the boundaries so neither of us really knows what they are.
Oh, OK I suppose you can do that. I don't really mind.

I **win**
You **win**   We can get along and get more of what we *all* want by operating within reasonable boundaries that are realistic to the situation. Instead of resisting and focusing on what we *can't* do, we focus on the many things that we *can* do and *want* to do within the boundaries. Let's focus on how situations can work in some way for *all* of us.
Let's play quietly while granddad watches the news.

The last way, **win-win**, is the most reasonable and respectful approach to adopt and is embodied in the following method.

The method

The boundary

Decide what boundaries you want for you and your family in your home. Discuss and agree these with any other adults who will be responsible for maintaining them. Make sure your boundaries honour both your children's needs (**Happy Kids**) and your needs (**Happy You**). State them in positive language, telling your children what they can do. Be aware of the limit set by a boundary, which will be expressed as a **don't**.

The positive consequences

Work out what the positive consequences (the benefits) are for having the boundary.

The negative consequences

Decide what the negative consequences will be for going beyond the boundary. Make sure you're prepared to follow through on these consequences and in a timeframe that keeps the association with the boundary clear to your child.

Positive language to support what they can do

Use positive language to tell your child what they can do. Encourage and support them in finding behaviours that are appropriate within the boundary.

The warning, followed by the choice

When a boundary is being seriously challenged, warn your child of the negative consequences. Follow up this warning immediately by offering your child the choice of the negative or positive consequences. State the positive consequences last (for emphasis) and make them sound really appealing.

Follow through

If your child then chooses to cross the boundary, follow through with the negative consequences. Otherwise, be impressed by their appropriate behaviour within the boundary and reinforce the associated positive consequences. (The **Be impressed** method, page 51, covers ways of giving effective praise.)

Here's an example:

The boundary

> We **don't** shout at the meal table while we're eating.
> We **do** talk to each other in our normal voices as we eat.

The positive consequences

> We enjoy eating and chatting together as a family at mealtimes.

The negative consequences

> We go and shout in the hall until we are ready to talk normally again.
> We may miss out on our meal if we spend too long shouting on our own in the hall.

Positive language to support what they can do

> Please use your normal voice so that I can hear you properly.

The warning, followed by the choice

> If you want to shout, you need to go in the hall.
> Do you want to go and shout in the hall or enjoy your tea here with us?

Follow through

> If you want to shout, go to the hall now please. You can come back when you're ready to talk normally.

> (If my child won't go on his own, I will carry him firmly and calmly to the hall. I use different negative consequences, such as removing privileges like pocket money, for my older children.)

Tips for good results

✓ Your boundaries may well be different from what you experienced as a child or what your friends do. That's OK. Children are very flexible and easily accept that different boundaries and rules apply in different environments, e.g. grandma's house, school, the swimming pool. What's important is that you and your family know how your boundaries work in your home. This also helps you deal with feedback from others who may comment on these differences.

✓ Boundaries need to be adjusted as you, your child and all your needs change over time. It's an ongoing process. As circumstances change, use the same six step method to define the new boundaries.

✓ As your children get older, involve them in family discussions about the boundaries that operate in your home. Two points to note though:
- The discussion happens at a time when everyone is calm, not when they are in the thick of challenging a boundary!
- As the responsible adult, you have the final say. Accept that you will be unpopular at times because your children will not always agree with or like the boundaries you need to set and that's OK. You have to hold and honour what you see as the long term benefits for your children.

✓ Accept that your children will challenge the boundaries. It's normal and healthy; it's their way of finding out how relationships and the society they live in work.

✓ When a boundary is being challenged, try to keep your enforcement role as impersonal and unemotional as possible; you are simply maintaining a boundary that defines "how we do things in this house". Depersonalising a challenge in this way really helps you to stay calm. (You may find the **Move beside** method, page 63, useful here.)

✓ Avoid using words such as "discipline", "punishment" or "reward". These words can feel too personal, too much like you're enforcing your will and power over your child and making it a **win-lose** situation.

✓ Accept that **win-lose** will occasionally happen; you are only human! Sometimes it is the best you can do when life and your children test you and the boundaries to the limit… and beyond.

✓ Although occasionally having to enforce reasonable boundaries is part of being a parent, you can think of it more generally as maintaining a space, environment and atmosphere which enable you and your family be your "best" selves.

More challenging situations

Now you have a go

Jot down some of the boundaries you maintain in your house.

- How realistic and reasonable are they?
- Do they honour both your needs and your child's needs?
- How have you worded them? Are they **don'ts** or **do's**?
- Make sure that all the **don'ts** have corresponding **do's**.
- What are the positive consequences for all concerned?
- What are the negative consequences should your child cross the boundary?
- How will you warn them and carry out any sanctions necessary?
- Remember to offer your child the choice of the negative or positive consequences; state the positive consequence last, as this is the option you would prefer them to choose.

And finally...

Your way or my way? If we're working your way, I can feel my views have not been taken into consideration and vice versa. So let's agree the "House Rules" for our home: the rules we all agree to live by that support most of our needs and wants most of the time. **Win-win**!

How this method worked for...

Rebecca

One week, during our 2-year-old's regular swimming class, he decided that he didn't want to join in with any of the activities. He was shouting and kicking and beginning to disturb the other children. As he was challenging the boundary of acceptable behaviour in his swimming lesson, I offered him the choice of the negative or positive consequence, positive last: we could either get out, get changed and go home, which would be rather boring. Or, if he settled down, we could stay in the pool, he could join in with the activities and have some fun. He calmed down almost immediately and we continued the lesson. He participated in all the exercises, laughing and giggling. We both had a brilliant time!

Result!

Sara

My 3-year-old loves tick charts as long as she can stick the ticks on our homemade chart. I use this as a positive consequence to keep her focused on various tasks, particularly getting washed and dressed. As she completes a task in a helpful, cooperative way, she gets to put a sticker on her chart against the symbol for that task. We take time to look at all the lovely stickers on her chart, showing how helpful and cooperative she is and increasingly how much she can do for herself.

*For a while, she really wanted to put her own toothpaste on her brush so I would ask "Would you like to put your toothpaste on your brush today?" to **Get a "Yes!"** (page 45) and get her to go upstairs to the bathroom. This developed into both my children (the other is 5) rushing upstairs to clean their teeth together. Fantastic! However, they then became increasingly distracted and playful after the excitement of toothpaste and wouldn't get on with washing and dressing.*

*I reconsidered how we were doing things and told them we were changing the order so that they cleaned their teeth **after** they had washed their faces. I also altered the order of the tasks on the tick chart to reinforce this change. This is currently working well and I'm intrigued to know what the next change will be to keep things running smoothly as their needs and capabilities change.*

Result!

Leanne

We wrote down some positive "House Rules" for the family: rules which we decided on together as a family and regularly refer to in our kitchen. These are a great focus for us all to work together. The atmosphere seems a lot more positive having these in place.

Result!

More challenging situations

Give and take: the *dance* of responsibility

5

Have you noticed how young children are usually determined to do things for themselves: "Me do it!" They are programmed to have a go, whether they can do it or not!

This is how children learn and we want our children to explore and learn to do things for themselves. Ultimately, we want them to become independent adults, completely responsible for themselves and their lives. And yet at birth our children are completely dependent upon us. So, in raising our children, we go from having **all** the responsibility for them, right through to the other extreme of having almost **none**.

Between these two extremes, over the years, there is a kind of *dance* of responsibility. It's a dance of give and take, of to and fro between parent and child as children take more and more responsibility overall for themselves. As a parent, you have to judge moment by moment when you need to step in to guide, help or take control and when it's best to step back and let them work things out for themselves.

This *dance* of responsibility can often lead to conflict. For example:

Your child wants to do something for themselves

> **vs.**
>
> For whatever reason, you cannot let them. Perhaps you don't have enough time, it's too dangerous or you know what happened last time.

Or

You want or need your child to take responsibility for doing something well within their capabilities

> **vs.**
>
> They won't!

You can often end up feeling cross and frustrated with yourself and your children.

Here's a method to help you feel more confident and assured about the level of responsibility you are giving and taking in a situation involving your children.

The method

This method helps you to first gauge the level of responsibility you are currently taking for your child, and then to adjust it as necessary.

Notice the level of responsibility you are currently taking for your child and what they are doing. This will range from

all - - - - - - - - - - - - - - - - - - through to - - - - - - - - - - - - - - - **none**

Where you are taking all the responsibility for your child

Where your child has taken responsibility for themselves

Now consider:

Are you taking too much responsibility?

Perhaps you are taking over, trying to control too much and not really "tuning in" to what your child is trying to do.

> **Suggested action:**
> *Step back* to allow your child more "space" so they can take responsibility. In the tips below, you'll find suggestions for methods that will help you do this.

Are you giving your child too much responsibility?

Perhaps you are expecting too much of your child and realise they need more guidance, support, control. Or even rescuing.

> **Suggested action:**
> *Step in* and take back some responsibility: get more involved in what your child is doing. Many methods will help you do this, as suggested in the tips below.

Have you got it *about right?*

In this case, things are either going really well or perhaps you are enforcing a boundary calmly and clearly, as your child experiences some negative consequences resulting from their actions.

> **Suggested action:**
> Either way, feel confident and reassured about your judgement and capabilities as a parent. **Be impressed ... with you** (page 153).

Here are some examples:

You notice your child putting her shoes on really, really slowly and you are about to take over and do it for her. You realise that this would be **taking too much responsibility** at this moment because there are other things you can usefully do to give her more time. You *step back* so that your child can get on with what she is doing.

Your toddler stumbles, falls over and starts wailing. You are about to go and comfort him when you judge that, for this minor fall, you would be **taking too much responsibility** for his needs. Instead, you offer him words of comfort and encourage him to *come to you* if he needs a cuddle. By letting him decide whether or not he wants to come to you, you are **giving him responsibility** for recognising and meeting his own needs.

For the last few days, you have enjoyed your bedtime routine with your child. She has been focused on doing as much as she can for herself and you have really appreciated her efforts. You are looking forward to the same level of independence tonight but it rapidly becomes obvious that it isn't going to happen. You begin to feel frustrated, wondering *why* she won't get on with it. However, you then realise that your expectations are probably too high as your child is only 3 after all! So you simply **take more responsibility** and give her more help on this occasion. In doing this, you remain impressed with how she did things on previous nights.

More challenging situations

Tips for good results

✓ When you are taking too much responsibility, check out **Pause for thought** (page 139) to help you *step back* and give your child more responsibility. You can also **Offer effective choices** (page 39). Choices will encourage your child to decide what they want – an important step in taking responsibility.

✓ Many of the methods in this book will help you to *step in* and take more responsibility for what your child is doing in a useful way. In particular, check out **Set and maintain reasonable boundaries** (page 89). Also, **Join them in their activity** (page 69) will help you to get more involved in what your child is doing.

✓ Build your child's confidence and set them up to succeed by letting them take a level of responsibility appropriate to their current abilities. Give them enough responsibility to feel motivated and challenged but not so much that they feel overwhelmed or inadequate.

✓ It's good to notice your level of responsibility when things are going well. **Be impressed** (page 51) with what your child is capable of on a good day and give them some praise.

✓ Give your child *enough* responsibility so that they can experience consequences in *small* ways that are manageable for them and you. For example, your child insists that they don't need their mittens as you go outside on a cold winter's day. Even though you allow them to leave without wearing any, you put the mittens in your pocket just in case. When they complain that they wants their mittens, you point out how cold their hands are and how nice it will be to put their mittens on before they leave next time. You are then "surprised" to find their mittens in your pocket and let them put them on.

Over time, this enables your child to take responsibility for their actions based on their own experience. As the responsible adult, how much responsibility you allow your child is always based on your judgement in the moment. Allowing your child to experience *small consequences* doesn't mean you don't care; it does mean that you trust your child to learn for themselves.

✓ It's easy to take too much responsibility for your children when you have lost sight of your needs. Check out the methods in Section 3 to explore how to **Take care of YOU**, especially **Find your good mood** (page 169).

✓ As they grow older children learn to take more responsibility themselves. There are many measures and books on what to expect from children at different ages. However, think of giving and taking responsibility as an ongoing *dance* with your children. This is because levels of responsibility are moving, moment by moment, in accordance with your children's changing needs, moods and expectations, and indeed your own.

Now you have a go

In any situation involving your child, take a moment to notice the level of responsibility you are currently taking for them.

Think about situations where things are going well. This suggests you've probably got your level of responsibility about right. Consider:

- How much responsibility are you giving your child?
- How much responsibility is your child taking?

Be impressed with your child and what they are doing in this situation. Be impressed with yourself for gauging an effective level of responsibility.

Now think about situations that haven't gone so well. Gauge the level of responsibility you were taking for your child and what they were doing. Consider how adjusting it to either *step back* and take less responsibility or *step in* to take more could have given you better ways of dealing with the situation. How much responsibility do you want to take next time this situation or something like it occurs?

The more you practise gauging your level of responsibility, the more easily you will be able to notice and adjust it as situations change.

And finally ...

Develop balance, agility and flexibility in your dance of responsibility with your children. This is the movement and rhythm of your developing relationships with them.

How this method worked for ...

Mark

Whenever I ask my 3-year-old if she wants to do something, I can pretty much guarantee her answer will be "No", even if it's something I know she will really enjoy. At first, I took her at her word: we didn't go out or do very much and it was getting really dull. Then I realised I was giving her too much responsibility for the decisions we were making. I was being ruled by the words of a 3-year-old!

When I thought about it like this, I realised that her "No" was perhaps more about her wanting to continue what she was doing; it wasn't necessarily that she didn't want to do what I was proposing. I took back responsibility for deciding what we were going to do and stopped asking her as much. Now I often simply assume we will do what I am proposing.

I am still surprised at how she can be getting ready to go out whilst happily and calmly telling me all about how she doesn't want to!
Result!

Helen

I use "House Rules" and positive and negative consequences to encourage my 6-year-old to take more responsibility. I give her regular pocket money – which she loves to manage – for being generally helpful and cooperative throughout the week. In addition to her regular pocket money, I give her a fixed amount of extra money at the end of a week in which she has done particular tasks helpfully and reliably. Her current tasks are setting the table for breakfast while I make packed lunches and clearing and wiping the table after meals. However, she only gets the extra pocket money if she does this **every** *day of the week; miss a day and she doesn't get the extra.*

It's always her choice to take responsibility for doing these tasks helpfully and reliably, which she usually does. It's great to have a good helper.
Result!

Find a useful meaning

5

Suddenly you notice it's gone very quiet and, even though you're pretty sure you know where your children are, you start to have that feeling that they're up to something no good. You go looking for them and, sure enough, as you round the corner, you are taken aback by the scene that confronts you:

These situations challenge us: How am I going to clear up this mess? How am I going to take care of someone's injury, or damage to something personal or precious? How can I make sense of a situation that completely confounds or perplexes me?

In that moment of impact, we cannot help but understand the situation based on how it affects us. We are likely to jump to conclusions and make assumptions about what we think is going on. However, different people have very different experiences and understand the same situation in very different ways.

Knowing that the way you understand a situation is only one way of looking at it gives you the opportunity to consider whether your current meaning serves you well:

- Does it cause you to behave how you would want to?
- Does it get good results for you and your children?

When you notice that your immediate response isn't useful, you have the opportunity to think flexibly and **find a more useful meaning**; an understanding that will get better results for you and your children.

The method

When a situation challenges you, **Look**, **Think** and **Look again**:

Look at your immediate response, how the situation affects **you** in the moment of impact.

Acknowledge that your immediate response is valid: it makes perfect sense **to you**, at this moment, based on **your** experience of the situation.

Now **Think** what this response gets for you:

- **Is it useful?**
- **Does your immediate response get good results for you and your child?**

If your answer is **No**, put your immediate response to one side for a moment, so that you can:

TAKE 2

Look again at the situation with fresh eyes:

- **What do you see now?**
- **What else could this situation mean?**
- **What can you now find in this situation to get a more useful result for you and your child?**

More challenging situations

Here are two examples:

Example 1: You've set out poster paints and brushes at the kitchen table and your 2-year-old son has just started doing some painting. You turn away for a moment and, when you turn back, he's pouring paint onto his hands.

Look at how the situation affects you in the moment of impact: your immediate response.

Oh no! I'm really annoyed! Why won't he use the paint brushes?! He's covered in it! This was just meant to be a quick paint before tea. He gets paint everywhere... I just want to clear it all away NOW. I wish I'd never got him started...

Acknowledge that your immediate response is valid: it makes perfect sense to you, at this moment, based on your experience of the situation.

Yes, it's an unpleasant surprise to turn round and see my child with paint on him. It's a level of mess I wasn't expecting...

Now Think where this response gets you: Is it useful? Does your immediate response get good results for you and your child?

No. If I clear up now, he will get frustrated and I'll be even more annoyed.

When your answer is *No*, put your immediate response to one side for a moment, so that you can:

Look again at the situation with fresh eyes: What do you see now? What else could this situation mean?

He's not doing this to annoy me. He's actually having great fun exploring the paint with his hands. I've covered the table and he's wearing his overall, so it's actually quite manageable...

What can you now find in this situation to get a more useful result for you and your child?

Now he's got paint on him I suppose he could do hand prints before tea – maybe even foot prints too! When he's done, I can give him a bowl of soapy water at the table to wash with so that he doesn't have to move.

Example 2: You've been on the telephone and, now the conversation is over, it's very quiet. You wonder where your 3-year-old daughter is. As you walk into her bedroom, you see crushed breakfast cereal all over the floor with your daughter sat in the middle of it with her back to you.

Look at how the situation affects you in the moment of impact: your immediate response.

What is going on?! I'm livid! What a mess! Where has all this come from? I take my eye off her for a minute and there's mess, mess and more mess! Aaargh!

Acknowledge that your immediate response is valid: it makes perfect sense to you, at this moment, based on your experience of the situation.

Yes, I experience and deal with mess that I would never have dreamed of before I had children. It can be really frustrating at times…

Now Think where this response gets you: Is it useful? Does your immediate response get good results for you and your child?

No: all I want to do right now is shout my frustration at her, which I know will only upset us both. I need to count to 10…

When your answer is No, put your immediate response to one side for a moment, so that you can:

TAKE 2

Look again at the situation with fresh eyes: What do you see now? What else could this situation mean?

Now I've calmed down a bit, I can put "the mess" to one side for a moment. I just want to know what on earth she's doing. I am able to ask her more calmly. It turns out that she has taken cereal from the kitchen and crushed it in a bowl to give to her toys for their breakfast. Hmm… By keeping "the mess" to one side, I am able to stay calm…

What can you now find in this situation to get a more useful result for you and your child?

I explain the difference between real and pretend food to her. I explain that real food stays in the kitchen where we eat together. She helps me clean up and we find some pretend food for her to give to her toys.

Tips for good results

✓ Give yourself a pat on the back when you successfully use this method. You have overcome your immediate response, found a different, more useful response and got a good result – well done! (**Be impressed ... with you!** page 153, has more on how to give yourself effective praise.)

✓ At the **Think** stage, you may need a moment to calm down and gather yourself before you can put your immediate meaning to one side. (See **Pause for thought**, page 139, and **Calm down**, page 145, for ways to give yourself this thinking time.) Take this thinking time when you know your immediate response won't get anything useful for you or your child.

✓ When you find yourself acting on your immediate response and you realise it's not useful, be prepared to back down. Exercise your prerogative to change your mind and **find a more useful meaning**.

✓ Use this method to reflect on situations that you feel you've handled less than well and would like to handle differently next time. By exploring what else the situation could have meant and how you would have liked to respond, you are mentally rehearsing how you want things to go next time. Even though this situation will never happen exactly the same way again, similar instances tend to reoccur until you've learned how to deal with them effectively. Vicky explains how this worked for her at the end of this section (page 110).

✓ The **Look again** stage often involves **turning a Stop into Go** (page 33). Once you've acknowledged and put your immediate response to one side, you can often see when, where or how your child's currently unacceptable behaviour might be acceptable. You can then redirect their behaviour appropriately.

✓ If you're frequently finding it hard to deal with situations where your child is "up to no good", you may find it helpful to take some calm time to reflect and think more positively about your child. The next method **Clean up your thinking** (page 111) or **What you focus on is what**

you get (page 83) will help you to do this. Alternatively, perhaps you need to take some time for yourself to recharge your batteries. Check out Section 3 to **Take care of YOU**, particularly **Find your good mood** (page 169).

Now you have a go

Recall a recent situation with your child where you know your immediate response wasn't useful, for example, you were taken by surprise by what you discovered.

If you acted on your immediate response and didn't get a good result, work through the steps of the method to explore how you would like to respond more usefully next time a situation like this occurs.

Alternatively, perhaps you recognised your immediate response wasn't working and you were able to adjust your response to get a good result. If this is the case, work through the steps of the method to understand more about how you already do this. You will then be more consciously aware of how you monitor and adapt your immediate response and can try it out more often, in more situations. Also, be sure to **Be impressed** (page 153) with your ability to use this method effectively.

You can also learn to respond more flexibly by noticing how others respond and get different results. Be curious about how they do what they do:

- What do they see when they look at the situation?
- What do they pay attention to?
- What does the situation mean to them that enables them to respond in the way they do?

If their way of looking at things makes sense to you too, see what results you can get by thinking in that way. (There's more on how you can learn from others in **It's cool to copy!** page 193.)

And finally ...

It's only natural that you will have immediate reactions to situations that catch you unawares. There are plenty of those in family life! Recognising and acknowledging your immediate response for what it is – just one way of looking at it – enables you to look beyond for more useful perspectives, meanings and results.

You can also help your children find more useful meanings in challenging situations. First acknowledge that their current response makes perfect sense from their current perspective. You can then encourage them to explore the situation and see it in different ways to get more useful results for themselves.

How this method worked for ...

Denise

My 4-year-old was supposed to be getting washed and ready for school. I had nipped to the toilet and when I came out he had disappeared downstairs. I found him naked on the window sill apparently playing with a toy parachute. I was embarrassed at this display of nakedness in full view of the neighbourhood. I was also cross that he still wasn't dressed. I recognised that my immediate response was also fuelled by expecting to get cross with him because I often do in the morning, trying to keep him on task.

Acknowledging that my frustration was a valid response to this situation enabled me to realise that my frustration rarely produces anything useful – quite the opposite. This allowed me to put my frustration to one side for a moment. I instantly remembered that I had left this parachute on his chest of drawers the previous night on the way to hanging it downstairs. We had agreed it could go downstairs after he'd hung it in the way of his curtains at his bedroom window. Obviously, when he went to get his clothes from his chest of drawers, he had found it and got distracted into re-hanging it himself – which was why he was on the window sill!

I could now see that, from his perspective, he was being helpful, trying to hang the parachute. So I simply helped him to hang it. He then got back on task getting dressed without any further prompting from me.

I could so easily have got annoyed with him, which would have only wound us both up and really slowed us down. Instead, I now have a better appreciation of how easily things distract him. He's only 4! I also appreciate that I get distracted too – I could have re-hung the parachute straight away the previous night ...

Result!

Vicky

My daughter had just started school, and was initially only in school until after lunch. When we got home, I wanted her to change out of her school uniform. Of course, she didn't and this was regularly causing conflict between us.

One afternoon, I thought she had gone upstairs to change but, after it had been quiet for a while, I went to check on her. No sign of her anywhere in the house so I went outside to look for her. It was a fine afternoon and the garage door was open. As I rounded the corner, there she was in the middle of the garage floor, still in her school uniform, making mud pies!

My immediate response was anger and frustration at her apparent defiance, not changing out of her uniform and now getting it covered in mud! I acted on this response, crossly telling her that she shouldn't be wearing her uniform to make mud pies. I demanded that she go inside and get changed straight away. Whilst she eventually came inside and got changed, she didn't go out to play again and we were grumpy with each other for the rest of the afternoon.

*I wasn't happy with how I'd handled this situation. Putting my anger and frustration to one side and **looking again**, I could now see the situation differently, more from my child's perspective: she was completely absorbed in her game and totally unaware of what she was wearing. My appearance at the door, large and looming with the sun behind me, probably startled her. I immediately put her "in the wrong", looking down on her and telling her in a cross voice what she shouldn't be doing.*

*I realised how frightening and threatening I probably appeared to her – scary! I also realised that all my immediate response had served to do was to upset her and teach her how to "be naughty", making me cross by wearing her school uniform to make mud pies! **How useful is that?**!*

*When I considered how I would have wanted to respond, I knew I really didn't want to be scary; I did want to show respect for her and her perspective and knew that I could do this by **joining her in her activity**. From a position of really appreciating how much she was enjoying playing with the mud (which I also used to do as a child), I could have asked her, "What clothes are good to wear for being really messy?" This way, I would have encouraged her to learn for herself what clothes to wear for messy play. **Much more useful!***

*To date, this exact situation has never happened again. However, the experience enabled me to recognise my immediate response to "messy" situations with my kids and to understand why it's not useful to act on it. I can often now put it to one side **in the moment** to handle these situations more effectively and kindly.*
Result!

Clean up your thinking

Do you ever find yourself thinking less than positive thoughts about your children?

Why is she always trying to annoy her sister?

She's so rude!

Why does he try to wind me up?!

I'm worried she's not "normal"...

He is a nightmare!

In the face of undesirable behaviour and circumstances that challenge, confuse and perplex us, it's not surprising that we sometimes think the worst of our children. Whilst it's understandable that this happens, our negative thinking can actually reinforce undesirable behaviour: we get more of what we *don't* want. By understanding the basis of our negative thinking, we can learn how to **clean up our thinking** so that we get more of the useful, desirable behaviours that we *do* want.

In order to think negatively about our children, we have to interpret their behaviour in a negative way; we assume, or think we know, that their behaviour arises from negative intentions, motives or qualities on their part.

Here's an example: Imagine that you have a 2-year-old child and a baby. You notice that your child is being rough with the baby. Based on this behaviour, you think:

He's jealous of his baby brother and wants to hurt him.

You assume, or think you know, that your child has the intention of *wanting to hurt his baby brother* – a negative intention.

Based on this assumption, you try to keep your child away from the baby, making him play somewhere else.

The probable effect of this is that your child becomes increasingly physical and difficult to manage around the baby.

Whether your assumption about your child's intention is right or not, it influences you to behave in ways that reinforce it. In trying to keep your baby safe, you create situations that may actually encourage your child to feel jealous and behave more roughly towards you and the baby.
Result: You get more of an undesirable behaviour.

Now let's look at this example again, but this time making a different assumption. You notice that your child is being rough with the baby and this time you think:

He's fascinated by his baby brother and wants to play with him. He doesn't know his own strength.

So you assume, or think you know, that your child has the intention of *wanting to play with his baby brother* – a positive intention.

Based on this assumption, you encourage him to be gentle, showing him where and how to hold the baby gently and carefully. You show him how to find and "share" appropriate toys with his little brother.

The probable effect here is that, even though you still have to keep an eye on things, you notice how much calmer and more gentle your child can be with his brother. You also enjoy involving your child as much as possible in caring for the baby.

A different assumption leads to a different result; you are now creating situations that encourage your child to "play nicely" with his brother.
Result: You get more of a desirable behaviour.

Whereas negative assumptions about your child's intentions tend to reinforce undesirable behaviours, positive assumptions about your child's intentions tend to support and encourage desirable behaviours.

So how do you get from   to

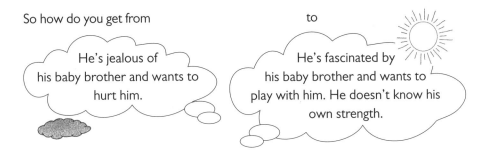

He's jealous of his baby brother and wants to hurt him.

He's fascinated by his baby brother and wants to play with him. He doesn't know his own strength.

The method

This method gives you three steps to change your assumptions and **clean up your thinking** to encourage and support desirable behaviour so that you bring out the best in your children.

 Step 1: Recognise your negative thinking

 Step 2: Find positive intentions

 Step 3: Encourage acceptable behaviour that fulfils positive intentions

Step 1: Recognise your negative thinking

It's natural to assume you know what your children's behaviour means. After all, this is how you learned to care for them from an early age. However, when you notice yourself thinking negatively about your children, recognise the limitations of your thinking:

- First, your assumptions may be wrong. Although you may think you know why your children behave the way they do, the reality is that there is no way of knowing what their intentions actually are unless you ask, understand and believe them!

- Second, regardless of whether your assumptions are right or not, thinking negatively about your children simply isn't useful: it plays no part in getting more desirable behaviour from them. In fact, it reinforces undesirable behaviours.

Discounting, or at least challenging, your negative thinking enables you to look for more positive intentions, motives and qualities. There is no harm in giving your children the benefit of the doubt and there are significant benefits to be gained.

Step 2: Find positive intentions

There are two ways to find positive intentions:

- for older children, you can **ask good questions**
- for any age child, you can **make positive assumptions.**

Ask good questions

For children who are old enough, you can find out what their intentions are simply by asking them. The following questions help you to bring out positive intentions and motives.

First ask: **What are you trying to do?**

A deceptively short and simple question! Depending on the circumstances, you may ask this question urgently, in a firm tone of voice, perhaps as you physically intervene to stop your child from hitting a sibling. Or perhaps, as your child's apparently strange

More challenging situations

behaviour baffles you, you ask it in a calm and curious tone of voice.

However you ask this question, it is vital that you:

- Listen to and seek to understand their response. They may not find it easy to explain in words, so give them time. If you don't understand something, stay curious and get them to clarify it.

- Accept and give credence to their response. Whilst you may doubt or not understand their intention, accept that it is important and means something *to them*.

Your child may not initially tell you their intention, so be prepared to ask this question more than once, until you get a sense of *what they are trying to do*.

Also, be ready to put a positive slant on a response that may, on the face of it, sound negative. For example,

Your child states   "I want my sister to go away"
to which you reply with   "Oh, you want to play by yourself right now…"

When you can put a positive slant on what they're trying to do, that's great. Go to Step 3. If you're struggling to find a positive slant, you can also ask:

Why is this [your child's intention] important to you?

or   **What does that [your child's intention] get for you?**

These questions seek to find a more general intention behind your child's first stated intention. For example, your child may want to be alone, or to be with others; they may want to stay in their internal world, or join in with what you're doing in the everyday world. It's often easier to put a positive slant on intentions which are more general, so ask these questions as many times as you need to, to find an intention that you can support.

Make positive assumptions

For children of any age, however bizarrely they behave, however unpleasant or misguided their behaviour may seem to you, making positive assumptions about their intentions enables you to engage with them in a useful way. Assume:

Everything anyone does has an underlying positive intention.

This general working assumption gives you the opportunity to find positive interpretations of what is happening.

To think positively about what your child's intention could be, ask yourself:

How can I interpret my child's behaviour in a useful way?

Why is it important to them to behave like this?

What does their behaviour get for them?

The positive intentions that you come up with will give you the basis for taking further action. When you have found a positive intention you can agree with, go to Step 3.

Examples of **positive intentions** include wanting to:

> play with a sibling
> help a sibling
> keep special toys or constructions safe
> be comfortable
> be safe
> have fun
> have a turn with a toy
> show a sibling how a toy works.

Step 3: Encourage acceptable behaviour that fulfils positive intentions

Now that you have a positive intention for your child's undesirable behaviour, you can help your child find a more acceptable way of fulfilling this intention.

Again, with older children, you can ask questions based on their positive intention to help them find their own new ways forward. For example:

Intention:	**Ask:**
Your children want to play together with the same toy.	What game can you play with this toy so that you're both happy?
Your son wants to keep his model safe from his little sister.	What would you like to do so that your model is safe?

With younger children, you can make suggestions as to how they can fulfil their intention. It's often worth asking them first though as they may surprise you with their ideas and resourcefulness!

Here are two examples:

Example 1: This summarises the example used in the introduction to this method. You have a 2-year-old child and a baby. You notice that your child is being rough with the baby. You've tried keeping your child away from the baby but it just seems to make things worse.

Step 1: Recognise your negative thinking.

You recognise that you've been assuming that he's jealous and is trying to hurt his baby bother. You realise that these assumptions are not working; you're unintentionally making him feel jealous.

Step 2: Find positive intentions by making positive assumptions
You ask yourself:

How can I interpret my child's behaviour in a useful way?
and realise that your child is fascinated by his baby brother and wants to play with him.

More challenging situations

Step 3: Encourage acceptable behaviour that fulfils positive intentions

Your new thinking leads you to trust that your child has positive intentions and motives. You now involve him as much as possible in looking after his baby brother. You show him how to be gentle and calm with the baby. Although this still has a challenging aspect, you're on the way to enjoying a real sense of "family time" as the three of you are all involved together.

Example 2: You have a son and a daughter aged nearly 4 and 2. They have been playing separately and happily on their own when you hear them arguing and, as you come to see what's going on, you see your son roughly push his younger sister over backwards and she starts to wail.

As you comfort your daughter and firmly tell your son, "That's too rough. We treat each other gently in this house," you are worried that your son is becoming overbearing and bullying his sister. You **recognise this negative thinking (Step 1)** *about your son so you ask:*

"What are you trying to do?" (Step 2: Ask good questions)

He says: "She's trying to take my truck."

You nod and acknowledge this, "Oh, I see," and ask again:

"What are you trying to do?"

He says: "I'm putting all my trucks together."

You notice he has lined up all his favourite trucks.

You make the following **positive assumptions (Step 2):**

- *My son wants to play with his favourite trucks and keep them safe.*
- *My daughter has played really well by herself and now wants some attention: she wants to play with her brother.*
- *My children often enjoy playing together so perhaps they would both enjoy playing together now.*

Encourage acceptable behaviour that fulfils positive intentions (Step 3):

To support all of the above intentions, you try asking your son

"What game can you both play with your trucks?"

He looks surprised for a moment and then thoughtful. He offers his digger (currently one of his less favoured vehicles) to his sister and says that she can "dig the gravel". Your daughter is delighted to be given something by her brother and immediately starts pushing it around. From here, your children play happily alongside each other for a while.

Tips for good results

✓ Make sure you ask **"What are you *trying* to do?"**

This question, in almost whatever tone of voice you ask it, invites your child to open up and reveal their intention.

Whereas   **"What are you doing?"**
and   **"Why are you doing that?"**

tend to imply disapproval, challenging your child to justify themselves and their behaviour. This may cause your child to feel under threat and become defensive.

✓ You can use the two parts of Step 2 (**Ask good questions** and **Make positive assumptions**) together to find your child's positive intention. This is because taking a moment to ask a good question also provides a **pause for thought** (page 139): an opportunity for you to think differently and make more positive assumptions. And vice versa: thinking positively about your child's intentions makes you more open and curious about their behaviour so you're more likely to want to ask them about it.

✓ Children often simply want attention (Don't we all?!). They want us to notice them, listen to them, play with them. They want to be with us, involved in what we are doing. Thinking of these as a valid, positive intentions leads us to find ways to include and involve them, giving them positive attention in useful, happy time together. Time like this builds

More challenging situations

your child's confidence and security to be apart from you and explore independently for a while. They are then less likely to challenge you and demand your attention in a negative way.

✓ When looking for your child's positive intentions, it can help to discuss this with a friend or partner, someone who knows and thinks well of your child. Keep your ideas and suggestions positive.

✓ Focusing on your children's positive intentions, motives and qualities supports and encourages them to behave in correspondingly desirable and useful ways. Use **Be impressed!** (page 51) to draw attention to and really enjoy the best in your children.

Now you have a go

Think of a situation where your child's undesirable behaviour has challenged you and you weren't happy with your response. Recall what you were thinking about your child in that situation.

- What assumptions were you making about their intentions and motives?

- How did these assumptions limit your ability to respond usefully?

- Assuming that "Everything anyone does has an underlying positive intention", what positive intentions can you now see that might have been underlying their behaviour?

- How would holding a positive intention in mind cause you to respond differently to this situation?

Consider how you can respond differently next time this behaviour occurs.

Here are some examples of how other parents have explored their negative assumptions to find more useful, positive assumptions about their children's behaviour. Cover up the right hand column and practise **cleaning up your thinking** by asking yourself:

How could I interpret this behaviour in a useful, positive way?

Negative interpretation	Positive interpretation
ignoring me	focused, absorbed, blissfully unaware
making a mess	learning new skills, exploring
easily distracted	curious, open to experiences
stubborn, fixated	determined, tenacious
challenging, pushy	opportunist, good negotiator
daydreaming	relaxed, calm, quiet

More challenging situations

And finally ...

This method is not suggesting that you should accept or condone undesirable behaviour. It is suggesting that you can separate what you think about your child and their intentions from what you think about their behaviour.

You can compound undesirable behaviour by thinking negatively about your child, seeing *the worst* in them. Alternatively, you can help your child find new more useful ways of behaving by **cleaning up your thinking**, seeing and trusting *the best* in them.

How this method worked for ...

Tom

*I was on a walk in the woods with my son and he ran on ahead. I came upon him hitting a plastic bottle with a stick. I was taken aback by the apparent violence and fierceness of his behaviour but had the presence of mind to ask, "**What are you trying to do?**" He replied, "I'm playing a tune!"*

It took me a moment to adjust to this new insight into his behaviour! I then encouraged him to explore the different sounds he could make by tapping the bottle more gently and using different, smaller sticks, more like drum sticks. We then went on to do a bit of litter tidying too!

It constantly amazes me how wide of the mark I can be in terms of what I think my children are trying to do! Sometimes, I find it really hard to believe what they say but I always seem to get a better result when I remember to ask, "What are you trying to do?"
Result!

Liz

*It was the end of bath time. My child was playing and she didn't want to get out so I gave her a "two minute warning". After a minute or two, I began to empty and remove the tubs she'd been playing with in the bath, putting them on the side to drain. As I pulled the plug out, she started putting the tubs back in the bath! In that moment, I interpreted her behaviour as blatant defiance of my authority. I was on the verge of "getting heavy" with her when I realised that this was my interpretation of her behaviour. I might be wrong ... so, in a less than friendly tone, I asked her, "**What are you trying to do?**"*

She replied, "I'm washing the bubbles out of the tubs." Whilst I found it hard to believe her response and saw it more as a delaying tactic, I no longer felt she was directly challenging me. Instead of "getting heavy", I told her to hurry up washing the tubs so she could get out, which she did.

I could so easily have got cross with her; it was the end of the day and I was feeling tired and hungry. The situation could then have escalated with me ultimately losing it. Noticing the assumptions I was making about her behaviour and remembering to ask her what she was trying to do diffused my tension enough to enable me to stay reasonable and calm, getting the kids off to bed relatively smoothly and happily.

Result!

Fiona

With the arrival of our first baby, I became really sleep deprived, up and down most of the night feeding and settling her. On several occasions in the small hours, I found myself silently cursing her for crying yet again and wondering why she was doing this to me, trying to drive me nuts! When I learned that **every behaviour has a positive intention**, I was able to see that crying was the only way she had of expressing her needs, whatever the time of day!

So obvious really but in my stressed out, sleep deprived state, I needed a way to "make sense" of it. Assuming positive intentions, even when I didn't know what they were, helped me to do this. From then on, keeping positive intentions in mind made it easier for me to tune in and interpret my baby's needs. I also became more accepting of myself and my needs; I was trying my best!

Result!

Find out what your body knows

In the Western world, we place great importance on using our heads to work things out, by analysing, rationalising and using logical thinking. This works very well much of the time. However, sometimes, our children and their behaviour really do our heads in: try as we might, we just can't work them or their behaviour out. The more we think about it, the more we get stuck in our heads.

This is when it's helpful to know that, in addition to our heads, we can use *our bodies* to understand our children better. Matching (page 75) summarises how to make a good connection with your child by copying their physical presence as closely as possible. You can also **join them in their activity** (page 69), "tuning in" to get a real sense of what's going on for your child in *their world*.

Usually though, when challenged by your child's strange or undesirable behaviour, the last thing you want or feel able to do is to match them or join them in their activity. However, there is nothing to lose and everything to gain from *trying it out later*, in a moment of calm and privacy, to **find out what your body knows**.

By pretending to be your child for even just a few moments, "stepping into *their* shoes", adopting their posture and role playing their behaviour, you can gain valuable new insights and understanding into why they do what they do.

Although this may sound like a bizarre, daunting or just plain silly thing to do, once you've tried it you realise what an amazingly quick and effective way it is to find out more about what's going on for your child. Actors use techniques like this to get into role, to explore the motives and thinking of the characters they're playing. You too can immediately get a better idea of the intentions and thinking that may be driving your child's behaviour. Then, the next time the situation arises, you can help them find more acceptable ways that fulfil their positive intentions as described on page 117.

The following method gives you a structure for using your body to explore your child's perspective in a challenging situation. In addition to your perspective and your child's perspective, this method also gives you a third perspective on the situation: that of a neutral observer or "fly on the wall".

The method

You will need 15–20 minutes of calm time to go through this method. You will also need enough space to have three distinct positions to move around, as shown:

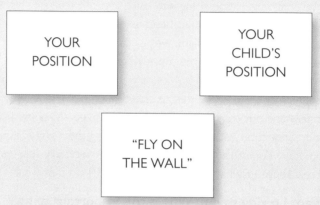

Your position represents **you** in the situation

Your child's position represents **your child** in the situation

The **"fly on the wall"** position gives you the opportunity to observe yourself, your child and what's going on between you. This position needs to be separate from you and your child, so you can see them both equally well.

The situation:
Think of the situation involving your child that you found challenging. For a recurring undesirable behaviour, think of a recent situation when your child behaved in this way.

Start in your position and relive the situation from your perspective. Notice what you see, hear and feel. This will feel quite natural because it's what you normally do. Look at your child's position and imagine that you can see your child there, as you saw them in that situation. Pay particular attention to their posture, physical movements and facial expression. Notice what you are thinking and feeling about your child as you look at them.

YOUR POSITION

Move out of your position, leaving all **your** thoughts and feelings about the situation behind you in this space. Have a little shake to loosen up – literally shake off your perspective of the situation.

YOUR CHILD'S POSITION

Move into your child's position and pretend to **be** your child. Adopt their posture, physical movements and facial expression as closely as you can. This may feel quite strange at first because it is an unusual thing to do. That's OK. Concentrate on what you're doing with your body in being your child. As you get into role as your child, consider:

- **What is this situation like for me (as my child)?**

- **What do I see, hear, think and feel?**

- **What am I trying to do? Why is this important to me?**

Move out of your child's position when you are ready, leaving all that you now know about **your child's experience** behind you in this space. Have another little shake to loosen up and shake off your child's perspective of the situation.

YOUR CHILD'S POSITION

"FLY ON THE WALL"

Move into the "fly on the wall" position. In this position you are a neutral observer or "fly on the wall". From here, you can look at both yourself and your child in that situation and also notice what's going on between you. Take as long as you need to absorb what you are now aware of from this neutral position.

YOUR POSITION

- **What advice can you give yourself, back in your position?**

Return to your position, to "your shoes", taking with you all that you have learned from the other positions.

More challenging situations

- **What do you now think and feel about your child and their behaviour?**

- **What do you want to do differently next time the situation occurs?**

Continue to use the positions to explore the situation further if you need to. You can also practise what you will do differently next time from your position. Always finish this method by returning to "your shoes" in your position.

Here's an example:

The situation:

My daughter is 3½, my son 1½. My daughter always seems to be "muscling in" on my son, taking over whatever it is that he is playing with. I'm worried that my daughter is becoming a bully. Only yesterday, when they were playing with building bricks, she kept taking the pieces that he was playing with and got annoyed when he wanted them back. I then got annoyed with her because she wouldn't give them to him.

```
┌──────────────┐
│    YOUR      │
│  POSITION    │
│              │
└──────────────┘
```

Starting in your position:

Reliving this situation from my position, as I look at my daughter, she's moved in front of my son and is taking building bricks out of his hands. She is very focused on the bricks and very forceful in her movements and voice tone. I feel cross with her and just want her to "share nicely". I don't really want to pretend to be her but I'm willing to have a go…

Moving into your child's position:

As I "step into my daughter's shoes", and start to role play her behaviour, I'm immediately aware of how fascinated I am by what my brother is doing. I want to show him how the bricks fit together because he's doing it all wrong.

```
┌──────────────┐
│    YOUR      │
│   CHILD'S    │
│  POSITION    │
└──────────────┘
```

This immediately triggers my adult thinking: I'm reminded of what it feels like to watch someone making a "bad job" of something. I would be itching to show them how to do it better and might take over without realising, just like my daughter is doing now!

Aha! Back in "my child's shoes", as my daughter, I realise my positive intention is to help my brother by fitting the bricks together for him!

Move out of your child's position:

*I'm surprised how quickly and easily I appreciated more about my daughter's perspective by **being** her in "in her shoes".*

"FLY ON
THE WALL"

Moving into the "fly on the wall" position:

From this objective viewpoint, I now see why my response in this situation hasn't been helpful. When I think that my daughter's intention is to help her brother instead of muscling in, I can come up with more useful ways to handle the situation.

What advice can you give yourself, back in your position?

Just as I would try to sit on my hands and be patient while watching someone else trying to do something, I want to encourage my daughter to help her brother by watching what he is doing and being impressed with his efforts. I also want to show her how to interest her brother in something and give it to him, particularly if he's got something that she wants. She can then have what she wants when he loses interest in it.

YOUR
POSITION

Returning to your position:

Back as myself in this situation, I immediately want to drop down to my daughter's level, beside her, so that we can watch her brother together. I can then help her see what he's trying to do and we can be impressed together. I can also show her how to interest him in other things.

I'm practising doing this now to get a feel for how it will work the next time this kind of situation happens.

More challenging situations

Tips for good results

✓ Get into role as much as possible. The more closely you match your child's body posture and facial expression and role play their undesirable behaviour, the more you'll find out about what's going on for them. New information opens up possibilities for responding more usefully to their behaviour.

✓ Although this method cannot give you certainty about what your child is thinking and feeling in a challenging situation, it can open up your thinking, giving you much more of an idea of *their* perspective.

✓ When using this method, have the positive intention of wanting to get more useful results for your child and yourself in this situation. Treat the information you gain in "their shoes" with respect and compassion because you are potentially connecting with your child's innermost thoughts.

✓ You can also use this method to explore situations involving more than one child. Decide which child's perspective you want to explore first and put them into **your child's position**. Once you have completed the method for this child, simply repeat the method using a *different* physical location to represent a different child's perspective in the situation.

✓ This method is also great for exploring relationships and challenging situations with adults.

Now you have a go

As you become familiar with this method, make sure you have enough calm time and space to work through the steps. As you move around the three positions take this book with you if you need to, to guide you through the steps.

If possible, go to the place where the situation you want to explore actually happened. Go to your position and your child's position in the spaces they occurred. Then find a convenient "fly on the wall" position from where you can neutrally observe what's going on between you and your child.

When moving to your child's position, to "step into your child's shoes", make sure that you have completely shaken off your feelings and thoughts from your position. If you feel reluctant about pretending to be your child or unconvinced about the point of it, this is still your adult thinking position. So shake those thoughts off too and enter into the world of your child which is free of these ideas. Go with it and role play your child as closely as you can. In this way you will **find out what your body knows**. Although at first it may take a little courage to pretend to be your child, think about how much time and head space it liberates – time you would have perhaps otherwise wasted by dwelling on your frustration with your child and their behaviour.

The more you use this method, the more you will find that the undesirable behaviour from your child doesn't personally challenge you so much. This is because you have become more curious and objective about their positive intentions that may be driving their behaviour. You may also find that you become more intuitive at reading your child's behaviour to find their positive intentions *in the moment*, so that you don't need to physically "be" them so much.

More challenging situations

And finally ...

As parents, we can find ourselves spending a lot of time and energy "in our heads", trying to work out the whys and wherefores of our children's behaviour. This method gives an alternative way to quickly gain more information, using our bodies to explore our children's point of view.

As the American Cheyenne Indian proverb says:

Do not judge your neighbour until you walk two moons in his moccasins.

There is nothing more respectful and useful in any relationship than trying to see the other person's point of view. So be *brave*: step out of your shoes and into your child's for a few moments. Be open to seeing a challenging situation through their eyes.

How this method worked for ...

Tracey

When my second child was 2 and having a tantrum, she developed a disturbing habit of curling up in a ball and banging her head on the floor. I found this very upsetting and difficult to deal with. I was concerned she would hurt herself (we have hard, concrete floors) and also concerned that maybe there was something wrong with her that I didn't understand. When I tried to stop her doing this, it only seemed to make her do it more. Eventually, in a moment of calm, I tried **finding out what my body knows***. I only had to go down into her mushroom position for a few moments to feel intense frustration at not being understood. I was trying so hard to express myself but couldn't make myself clear. I also realised that banging my head on the floor pretty much guaranteed I'd get some attention from Mummy.*

When I looked at myself and my daughter from the "fly on the wall" position, I could see how her behaviour was getting lots of negative attention from me. She became the focus of attention. I realised I needed to more consciously give her positive attention, patiently listening to her, staying calm and trying to understand what she was trying to communicate. I could also recognise and feel reassured by all the positive attention I was already giving her.

After using this method, whilst her head banging behaviour still disturbed me, I was able to try leaving her to it. I was very surprised at how much more quickly she seemed to sort herself out when left alone and, over time, I noticed she did it less often.
Result!

Jacqui

Once both my kids were at school, I missed them and really looked forward to picking them up from school in the afternoon. Sometimes they were happy and pleased to see me, but occasionally one or other of them would be grumpy and argumentative. The grumpy one would wind up the other one, which really wound me up. Before we knew it, we were all in a bad mood. This seemed to be happening more frequently, particularly with my younger son being horrible to his brother.

*I tried various methods to change this situation. With my youngest, I tried **getting down to his level** (page 59) and being patient with him, but he just wound me up first! I tried **adjusting my expectations** (page 177) so I wasn't expecting them to be nice when we met. Actually though, I really did want us to be nice to each other and didn't want to let go of that expectation. In desperation, I tried to **find out what my body knows**.*

*It felt weird to stand in my living room pretending to look at my son as he came out of school. I could immediately feel my delight at seeing him but I also noticed my anxiety about what mood he was going to be in. It was only when I stepped into his shoes and became him for a moment that I realised **why** he was in a bad mood: he was hungry!*

I usually take a couple of bananas down to school with me now. Once they've had a quick snack, my children are much nicer.

Result!

Putting it all together

The methods in this section have all focused on ways of thinking differently, of exploring challenging situations and behaviours from different perspectives. Gaining new information and insights into what's going on enables you to find new ways forward; new approaches that get more useful results for you and your children.

The last three methods have explored ways in which your current thinking may be limiting you:

1. When your immediate response to a situation doesn't serve you well, you can **find a useful meaning** (page 103).

2. When your assumptions about your children, their intentions and motives, are less than positive you can **clean up your thinking** (page 111).

More challenging situations

3. When you're stuck in your head and just can't work things out, you can physically explore your child's perspective and **find out what your body knows** (page 125).

These three methods overlap to some extent. They also resonate with the earlier three methods that explored how your thinking determines the environment and atmosphere you create in your home and your expectations of your children and their behaviour.

The methods in this section have been presented as distinctly as possible to give you as many options as possible to try something different in challenging situations. Remember, there is no right answer when it comes to parenting; what works today may not work tomorrow. What's important is that you continue to find and use what works for you and your children on a day to day basis.

The next section explores more of what's going on *on the inside* for you: your attitude and your mood. How are you meeting your own wants and needs to be *Happy You?*

Section 3

Take care of *YOU*

*Being the best you can be
for yourself and for your children*

Introduction

So far, the methods in this book have focused primarily on your children and your relationships with them. They have given you more choices about how to use your words, actions and thinking to get more of what you want in your family life. The focus has been:

SITUATION + YOU + Your CHOICES ⇒ RESULT
i.e. What happens next

But now, let's change the emphasis:

Situation + **YOU** + Your Choices ⇒ RESULT
i.e. What happens next

You become the most significant part of the equation! Your mood, your attitude, how you are feeling today, all have a huge impact on what you're thinking and then what you choose to say and do. Your words and actions then directly affect those around you, including your children, so it's essential to take care of yourself – both for your benefit and for the direct benefit of those around you.

In this section you'll find ways to recognise and meet your own wants and needs, to value yourself and to put yourself in a good mood more of the time. All these enable you to be more open and curious about what's going on around you. You'll be more aware of what you want and better able to recognise and take opportunities to achieve the results you want.

The methods are:

- Pause for thought
- Concentrate on something mundane
- Use peripheral vision
- Give yourself praise the *EASY* way
- Celebrate your successes daily
- Give yourself a *good* talking to
- Balance your needs into the mix
- Adjust your expectations.

Pause for thought

One morning, I was upstairs in the bathroom helping my two children get washed and ready for the day ahead. My elder daughter had just turned 3 years old and my baby daughter was about 10 months old. I was kneeling on the floor putting a nappy on her when my elder said, "Look! My black pen!" and showed me her black felt tip pen which she had just found on the window sill.

Seeing this pen immediately reminded me of how it came to be in the bathroom:

> A couple of weeks before, she had been having a tantrum, refusing to do anything towards getting ready for bed. At the time, we were using a sticker chart to encourage her to notice and enjoy how good she was at doing things for herself, like washing and dressing. The negative consequence of her being uncooperative was a black spot on her sticker chart! On this occasion, I'd had to bring her chart and her pen to the bathroom to put a black spot on it, which had thankfully got her moving again.

I was just about to say, "Yes, and we both know how that got here!" when I **paused** ... I realised that this would remind her of her bad behaviour and probably put us both in a bad mood. *Not the result I wanted!*

In the next moment, I noticed that my baby was starting to reach out and move towards the pen. I was just about to say, "Don't give her the pen!" when again, I **paused** ... I realised that this negative command would probably cause my 3-year-old to give the pen to her younger sister. *Not the result I wanted!*

I was in quite a good mood that day and the situation was quite calm. I was able to take advantage of my **pauses** to stop myself from saying things I knew wouldn't work. I was then able to say something neutral, which opened up the situation in a positive way.

What I actually said was, "Yes, your black pen. Where does that belong?" to which my 3-year-old replied, "Downstairs in the pen box." I then asked her to put it back on the window sill while we carried on getting ready. To my surprise and

Take care of YOU

delight, after we had finished in the bathroom, she spontaneously took the pen back downstairs and put it away.
Result!

The method

Aha! Notice when what you are doing isn't working, or when you are about to say or do something that you know isn't going to work. This is the moment when you have the opportunity to choose a better way forward.

Hold this moment as long as you need to, in order to:

- say or do something that you think will work (this is a great opportunity to use other *Happy Kids Happy You* methods you are familiar with)

- say or do something that feels more neutral

- do nothing! This can often be better than carrying on with what you know won't work. Doing nothing can sometimes yield surprising results. Sarah explains how it worked for her at the end of this section (page 143).

Sometimes, the situation and your mood are such that, despite knowing you're on a downward spiral, all you can do is plough on regardless. In this situation, accept you're doing the best you can and go for damage limitation. We all mess up from time to time. It's useful for your kids to see you make mistakes and to then see you learning from them, being and saying "Sorry" to those you affected along the way.

For situations that keep catching you out, you can do something now, before they happen again. Take some calm, child-free time to explore a challenging situation in order to gain new information about it. Use a method such as **Find out what your body knows** (page 125).

Tips for good results

Here are some suggestions that others have found useful to **pause for thought**. They may also help you to capture and hold the moment and give yourself chance to find a different, and better, way forward:

✓ Say to yourself: "Wait a minute …", "That's interesting …" or, "This too will pass …"

✓ Step back and/or adopt a thoughtful pose. This immediately puts you in a position to come up with and consider other options!

✓ Count to 10.

✓ Find a mirror and notice your "cross face". Now give yourself a warm, sympathetic smile! Even managing a cheesy grin will change how you're feeling! You're doing the best you can and it just got better!

✓ Take a long, deep breath in followed by an even longer, deeper sigh… This helps release physical tension, and this change in your physical state gives you an opportunity to change your thoughts.

✓ Shake your tension out, e.g. wave your arms and hands about, jump up and down on the spot, put on some music and dance about.

✓ Have a great big stretch, reaching up for patience and inspiration!

✓ Act as if a good friend – someone you respect, a mentor or role model – is with you in the situation. How does their presence change your mood and your thinking?

✓ Stick a ▐▐ symbol in your current "hot spot" for challenging situations. Put it where it will catch your eye to remind you to stay open to possibilities in this situation. You can also use sticky notes to remind yourself of the words you want to say or to give yourself a special message that will help and encourage you.

Take care of YOU

✓ Have a daydream, however fleeting!

✓ Walk away. Literally getting some distance changes your perspective on the situation.

✓ Shut yourself in a room (e.g. the toilet!), if only for a few moments, to give yourself some head space. If nothing else, it's symbolic and seems to help.

Although it's not always possible to do these things, once you give yourself permission to try them, it's surprising how many you *can* use when you need to, and this is by no means a comprehensive list. There are undoubtedly many more … What do you do already that works well for you?

And finally …

Give yourself a pat on the back when you recognise it's time to use a **pause for thought** in order to find a better way forward. You've just done something new and different that worked. Well done! (The **Be impressed … with you!** method, page 153, has more ways of giving yourself effective praise.)

However deep into a situation you have plunged, whenever you notice that what you are saying or doing isn't working, take a moment for yourself, however brief. Gather yourself and your thoughts so that you may return refreshed.

How this method worked for …

Jenna

One evening my husband was out and I was trying to get all three of my children to bed on my own. It was like a game where just when you get one ball in the right hole, another bounces out of its resting place! They all wanted my attention and no one was feeling sleepy and settled.

I went to the bathroom, screamed silently, and then paused and thought, "OK, what's really going on here? How can I read to all of them when they all want something different?"

The solution was remarkably simple. I asked my eldest to read to my youngest – "play Daddy" in return for a longer chat later. She loved the idea and put her heart and soul into The Gruffalo. Meanwhile I read to my son – he's always the quickest to go to sleep. With one down it's always easier to settle two. I joined the girls in time to act out the mouse wanting to sleep now the Gruffalo had gone and all was quiet. Two down! I was able to make my eldest feel really good about herself as she had been a great help. We chatted, she went to bed happy and so did I. My youngest often requests her sister to read to her now.

Result!

Sarah

One morning, my 4-year-old was being really demanding, wanting me to help her with everything and being quite obnoxious about it. She was really starting to get to me and I was about to "help" her, which I knew was only going to wind me up, when I noticed myself in the mirror.

I gave myself a great big smile and then winked at myself. I felt my whole body relax and it was as if I'd had a great big hug from a friend. In those few moments that I had with myself, my daughter started getting herself dressed!

Result!

Simon

One day, I could feel my anger rising within me and I knew I was going to lose it. I'm proud to say that I had the presence of mind to tell my children that, "Daddy needs to have a shout. I'm going into the lounge to have a shout…" This is where we usually send the children if they want to shout. I fled to the lounge and had my shout.

I felt much better for it and returned to the kitchen feeling calmer and more able to cope. The kids seemed to take this as being a perfectly normal thing for Daddy to do! I'm so glad that I let my anger out in a controlled way, away from my kids.

Result!

Take care of YOU

Take care of YOU

Calm down

Even when I woke up one morning, I was feeling completely exhausted. I had so little energy that I felt sure it was going to be a difficult day.

To my surprise, I found myself being really effective. Situations which on other days would have annoyed me and wound me up didn't get to me; I just didn't have enough energy to get annoyed! Because I could be nothing but calm, I was more open and responsive to what was going on. I was able to think more clearly and practically. Not only was I more effective, I also found that my behaviour was generally more respectful to my children and partner!

Although this experience convinced me of the value of being calm, I didn't want to have to go on being completely exhausted in order to get the benefits! Now, I don't consider myself to be a naturally calm or laid back person and I find it hard to chill out or go with the flow. So I realised I had some learning to do in order to find and use a state of calmness more often.

Genuine calm isn't a behaviour that you can *do*. It's an inner state of *being*, a mood, an openness of mind from which flows calm, reasoned behaviour. Indeed, trying to behave calmly when you don't feel calm can increase your inner conflict and tension. It's like shouting "I'm happy!" through gritted teeth!

Calmness is the combined effect of a physically relaxed body and a mentally relaxed mind. They feed off each other:

So, to **calm down**, you can
1. relax your body by removing physical tension
2. relax your mind by controlling your thinking
3. do 1 and 2 at the same time.

Physically relaxed body

Mentally relaxed mind

There are many ways of doing these to achieve varying degrees of calmness. They range from sustained practices such as meditation or physical relaxation techniques, right through to really quick, *in the moment* techniques, such as counting to 10. Different approaches work for different people at different times in their lives. You already know some ways that work for you to calm down. So here are some further methods for you to explore and adapt.

Take care of *YOU*

Concentrate on something mundane

The method

One way to calm down is by controlling your thinking. Deliberately occupying your mind with mundane thoughts effectively displaces other thoughts. Mundane thoughts are tension-free so occupying your mind with a mundane task prevents other more stressful or agitating thoughts from bothering you. Your body then follows your thinking: mundane thoughts lead to the release of tension so you become more physically relaxed.

Try these mundane tasks:

- Close your eyes and imagine clouds forming the number 100. Now have the clouds change to form the numbers 99, 98, and so on, counting down one by one.

- Focus on an object that you can see easily and comfortably, something that you find pleasing, such as a plant or a vase. Become fascinated by it and visually explore it in all its details.

There are many other common techniques, including counting to 10, counting sheep in order to go to sleep and recalling in detail a calm, tranquil scene.

After just a few moments of concentrating on your mundane task, you can notice how your breathing has slowed and tension in your body has been released. You may find yourself yawning or sighing deeply. You can deepen your state of calmness as you continue with your mundane task by becoming more aware of these pleasant effects on your body and your breathing. Your physical and mental states are feeding off each other, as described above.

Once your body has released some mental and physical tension, you have moved into a position of choice. Depending on the constraints of the situation you are in, you can choose to:

- Continue to deepen your level of calm. Either keep on with your mundane task or introduce any other method for relaxing that you know.

Take care of YOU

- Pick another *Happy Kids Happy You* method and apply it to the situation that's challenging you.

- Focus once again on what is going on around you. In choosing to do this, you've effectively taken a **pause for thought** (page 139).

 # Use peripheral vision

The method

Using your *peripheral vision* to calm down is quick and effective because it combines your thinking with the way your body works:

Your eyes are amazing pieces of sensory equipment. Whilst you may be directly focusing on something in front of you, you can also be aware of a visual field of almost 180 degrees in front of you. You can be visually aware of what's going on without needing to look at everything directly. This is peripheral vision: seeing without directly looking.

Consciously activating your peripheral visual awareness relaxes you and releases physical tension. Simply by changing your visual awareness from direct to peripheral will cause you to become calmer.

Here's one way to practise doing it:

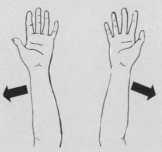

Put your hands together directly in front of you and look at them without staring. Now slowly move your hands apart, making sure you can see both of them equally. You can wiggle your fingers a little to reassure yourself that you are seeing each hand, even though you are not looking directly at either of them. Continue to move your hands apart slowly in an arc until they are just at the edge of your visual field. Take a moment and notice how your breathing has slowed and you have relaxed.

When you've practised doing this, you'll find you can switch into peripheral vision simply by focusing equally on two objects widely separated in your field of vision. Once using peripheral vision has released some mental and physical tension, you have moved into a position of choice. As with the previous method, you can either go into a deeper state of calm or refocus on what's going on around you, and contemplate using another *Happy Kids Happy You* method.

Some everyday examples of peripheral visual awareness:

- People commonly talk about noticing something out of the corner of their eye.

- People also talk about being miles away when they're daydreaming with eyes open but de-focused.

- Peripheral visual awareness is associated with high performance states, such as skiing, horse-riding and driving a car. A juggler also uses peripheral visual awareness very effectively to notice *enough* about the objects he is juggling without locking on to any single one. If you have more than one child, you may already be very familiar with this!

Tips for good results

✓ Calming down is key to unblocking states of emotional, mental and/or physical tension. If you are feeling stuck, stressed or angry, release the tension to improve your mood and open up your thinking to new possibilities.

✓ Beware of *acting* calm on the outside without being genuinely calm on the inside. Even though you may be able to pretend for a while, it's hard to maintain if you don't *feel* calm on the inside. Acting calm can even become a source of tension from the inner conflict it produces. If this is the case, **Giving yourself a *good* talking to** (page 163) will help you talk to yourself more calmly and supportively.

✓ Check out the **Pause for thought** tips (page 139) for more suggestions on quick ways to calm down.

Take care of YOU

✓ Take a few seconds, minutes or longer to calm down; however long you need to reap only benefits from more reasonable thinking and behaviour. These are very adaptable methods so make them your own: explore and find **your** ways to calm down.

Now you have a go

Choose a method which appeals to you and try it out. Don't give yourself a hard time if you're not immediately feeling calmer; that kind of thinking creates tension, which is the opposite to what you want! Take your time and if you find something isn't working for you, simply try something different. For instance, if you choose counting down from 100, and that's winding you up for whatever reason, try another mundane task. Do anything that you find relaxing and that requires very little thought.

When you're practising peripheral vision be gentle with yourself. It may take a while to get the hang of it.

Listen to the feedback your body is giving you and notice the little clues you get that indicate you're in a calmer state.

At first, it helps to be in a quiet space on your own with at least 2 minutes to get a feel for a technique. It helps if your posture allows you to breathe fully using your diaphragm so that your stomach is moving in and out. Typically, standing or sitting upright are best because they can be done in most situations. As you get more used to calming down, you'll be able to do it no matter when or where you are.

Practise and get familiar with knowing and using a state of calmness. **Practice makes permanent** (page 209) suggests how to incorporate a state of calmness into your daily life.

And finally...

Calming down changes your mood and your thinking. Being calm opens up choices for going forward, giving you different ways to use your energy more effectively.

Take care of YOU

How these methods worked for...

Concentrate on something mundane

Martin

When I experimented with counting down from 100 in clouds, I noticed my jaw was tight: it felt tight under my ears and my top teeth were touching my bottom teeth. I knew I was still tense. When I let my mouth hang open very slightly, I felt my cheeks drop and my breathing deepen. Then I felt much calmer and knew that I had released the tension. I now use focusing on my jaw as my "mundane task" to calm down. It works a treat!

Result!

Sally

I am a light sleeper and find it hard to settle back to sleep when I have been up to my children in the night. When I'm struggling to get back to sleep, I now know how to use my thinking to relax my body so that at least I can feel physically rested. I found this particularly useful when my children were babies and I was up and down several times in the night.

Result!

Use peripheral vision

Jo

I have four children aged between 2 and 8 so things can often get pretty tense and fraught. When I find myself getting stressed, I go to the bathroom and take just a few moments to go into peripheral vision and shift my awareness to my breathing. I immediately feel refreshed and calmer about what's going on. It's as good as a "power nap"!

Result!

Caroline

*Sometimes I find that family life just gets to me and I feel myself getting cross for no apparent reason. Now I recognise this feeling as a signal that I need some space to myself, even just a few moments to calm down and simply **be**. Since recognising this need in me, I have made a few moments of calmness part of my daily routine at the beginning and end of each day. I also switch to peripheral vision and use breathing awareness whenever I think of it to top up my calmness and feel at ease with myself.*

Result!

Be impressed ... with you!

One of the best ways you can look after yourself and build your confidence and self-esteem is to notice all the positive things you're doing as a parent. But how do you know when you've done well as a parent? How do you recognise and acknowledge a job well done?

It's only natural that we look for external signs from our children, family and friends that tell us we're doing a good job as parents. We may then judge ourselves and our performance based on how we rate this external evidence. But first, let's consider how this approach can limit us and prevent us from recognising and feeling good about what we're doing well. We'll then explore an alternative way to **be impressed with you**.

Do you rely on the appreciation of others?
Whilst others may indeed appreciate your contribution, all too often their appreciation may get lost in the hurly-burly of family life. If you rely on this feedback for your sense of being valued as a parent, you may feel dissatisfied and taken for granted.

Do you take the view that "the proof is in the pudding"?
Then you only really know you've done well when your children have grown up and succeeded in their lives. This view has some inherent pitfalls and dangers:

- Your sense of yourself and the value of your efforts rise and fall with the performance of your child. It's as if the jury's always out with regard to the value of your contribution as a parent.

- You can only recognise your success as a parent when your child has matched up to your expectations of them. When do you decide that your child has achieved *enough* for you to give yourself that pat on the back?

- You're tying your children into your opinions and beliefs about what "success" is in life. This makes it harder for you to be involved when they make life choices that do not concur with your opinions.

- When your children are "failing", you are failing too. If your child is not meeting your expectations, and is perhaps most in need of your unconditional love and support, you may not be able to give it because you are preoccupied with doubting your abilities as a parent.

Here's an alternative way of thinking:

Give yourself permission to feel good about the effort *you* are putting in: the things you do, day in day out, to keep the wheels of family life turning; the thought and consideration you give to your children, all with the intention of *bringing out the best in them and you*. Be actively impressed with yourself and the positive contribution you make as a parent. Do this *now* regardless of how you feel about the overall results, good or bad, immediate or long term.

Based on this way of thinking, the following two methods to **be impressed with you** have two major advantages:

- You're free from needing the appreciation of others. It's an added bonus when you get some!

- You can be more open to recognising and supporting your children being successful in ways that make sense to *them*, even though they may not make sense to you.

Give yourself praise the *EASY* way

  5

The method

Use the same *EASY* structure as given in the **Be impressed!** method (page 51) to give *yourself* effective praise. This is a great way to notice and acknowledge your successes *in the moment*.

Whenever you catch yourself being effective, doing a good job, ask yourself:

E What's the **Evidence?** Notice how your actions are producing something useful – a good result! How can you tell? What do you see, hear and feel?

A What specific **Action** have you taken? Notice what you're doing or what you've done. Use a kind, encouraging voice to tell yourself what this is. Also notice how you've done it.

S What does this **Say** or **Show** about **You?** Think about how your
Y actions demonstrate qualities that are important to you, e.g. helpful, kind, organised. Tell yourself how glad you are that you demonstrate and live these qualities.

Here are two examples:

You serve up a healthy meal for your family.

E

What's the *Evidence?*

Smells and looks great!

Take care of YOU

A

What specific *Action* have you taken?

I thought ahead to plan and prepare a healthy meal.

S
Y

What does this *Say or Show* about *You*?

I want all of us to know what healthy food is and to enjoy eating it. I care about my family.

You manage to get your child to go into his swimming lesson, despite his reluctance and protests.

E

What's the *Evidence*?

He's splashing about and really enjoying his lesson.

A

What specific *Action* have you taken?

I stayed calm and made sure he went in with his buddy. I'm sat here now ready to wave if he looks this way for reassurance.

S
Y

What does this *Say or Show* about *You*?

I'm aware of and sensitive to my son's needs. I know he'll be safe and have fun in the water.

Take care of YOU

Tips for good results

✓ When you catch yourself being effective in this way, jot it down or make a mental note as it's easy to forget the good things! Keep a running log through the day. A small notebook may help you do this. Refer back to it to reassure yourself when things aren't going so well.

✓ When others compliment you on your skills or qualities, accept and treasure these as a true reflection of how others see you. Believe them. You are indeed impressive.

✓ Check out the tips in the **Be impressed!** method (page 51). You can encourage yourself using these same tips that work for being impressed with your children. Your children need a pat on the back – so do you.

Now you have a go

Start by simply recalling a situation, any situation, where you did a good job as a parent. Write down what you did in your dedicated notebook or on a piece of paper.

Work through the **EASY** steps and really appreciate how well you did:

E   What's the **E**vidence?
A   What specific **A**ction have you taken?
S   What does this **S**ay or **S**how about
Y   **Y**ou?

Well done! It may feel artificial to do this at first, uncomfortable even. This is a good sign because you're trying out something new and different. If you value yourself in this way regularly over time, you will become more comfortable with the process. So stick with it; you're worth it!

Take care of YOU

And finally ...

Giving yourself praise, recognising and acknowledging your positive efforts as a parent, is a great way to build your own confidence and self-esteem. It's also a great way to demonstrate the kind of self-worth that you would like your children to have for themselves. (**Walk your talk**, page 185, has more about the role model you present to your children.)

How this method worked for ...

Maria
I'm feeling much better about myself as a parent, noticing what I'm doing well more often. I am more reassured that I'm doing a good job most of the time!
Result!

Gail
I love being impressed with my kids and being allowed to be impressed with myself! We have a lot more fun and know we're happy more of the time!
Result!

Rosie
I decided to record situations that I was really proud of onto my mobile phone. It felt really weird doing it at first, especially when I heard my own voice talking to me. I've got more used to it now and it's really useful to listen to when I'm feeling down or particularly useless. I'm getting used to listening to my own friendly voice and can hear it in my head more often now, telling me what I've done well and giving me encouragement. I enjoyed using the **Give yourself a good talking to** *method (page 163) to play with my "inner voice". I'm more aware of how I use my voice and what I sound like to others now.*
Result!

Celebrate your successes daily

The method

Spend 5 minutes every day doing the following:

- Find at least three recent examples of when you did a good job as a parent: moments, situations, conversations, events, choices you made, things you said or did. They could be anything from laughing at a joke to managing a complex, stressful situation. They could be times when things went really well for all concerned, right through to times when you know you did the best you could for your children in the long run, even though maybe you weren't too popular at the time!

- Think about how you were effective:

   What did you do?
   How did you do it?

   This really helps you acknowledge what you do that works with your children.

- Take time to enjoy these successes of yours. Give yourself a pat on the back: a reward for a job well done. Your reward could simply be taking the time to recognise what you've done well, or relaxing in the bath, enjoying listening to some music, a glass of wine or taking a day off! You know what's appropriate and what will work for you.

Here are some examples of daily successes:

I haven't raised my voice all day! I have used a reasonable, pleasant voice all day!

I enjoyed noticing my children encouraging each other. They learned that from me!

I took the kids to a party this afternoon, freeing up my partner to sit in the afternoon sunshine and read the paper!

I noticed myself being relaxed and happy! It's great! It's also great for my whole family!

I made the effort to do crafts with the kids. I let them get on with it (instead of being bothered by the mess they were making!) and tidied up afterwards.

I walked away instead of getting involved and wound up. When I came back, we'd all moved on.

I got back from work in time to say goodnight to the kids.

Tips for good results

✓ Small is beautiful! Obviously, major breakthroughs are fantastic when they happen but you can also find the smallest things to acknowledge and enjoy, as shown in the examples above.

✓ During your regular 5 minutes, record your daily successes in some way: perhaps write them in a journal or e-journal, email them to an understanding friend, record them on your phone or iPod – whatever works best for you. In this way, recognising and acknowledging your successes becomes a desirable habit. It also provides a record that you can turn to when things aren't going so well. You can remind yourself how impressive you have been in the past and will be again!

✓ Recognise what comes naturally to you such as methods in this book that you looked at and thought, "That's obvious. I do that already." Enjoy this. Well done!

Now you have a go

Decide what time of day will work best for you to take 5 minutes to reflect on your successes. Decide where you want to be to do this: a comfortable, calm and quiet spot is preferable. If you want to record your successes as recommended in the **Tips for good results** above, decide how you want to do this so that you have what you need ready to use.

When you first have a go at doing this, you may feel uncomfortable and perhaps self-indulgent. As with the previous method, this is a good sign because you're trying out something new and different. Initially, you may also find it challenging to think of things you have done well. *Remember, small is beautiful*: your success can be something as simple as smiling. Once you have come up with one thing, however small, you will be surprised at how easily other examples start to come to mind. The more the better! Jot them all down.

Get into a daily habit of **celebrating your successes**. This builds your self-esteem and confidence and improves your mood. Commit to taking 5 minutes every day for the next ten days to write down at least three examples of your successes to find out just how well it works for you.

And finally...

Both of these methods are great ways to choose to focus on what you're doing well. And remember, **What you focus on is what you get** (page 83). So focusing on your effectiveness means you'll be more effective more of the time. Giving yourself permission to feel good about yourself produces great results!

How this method worked for...

Andrew

*This evening, instead of getting exasperated by my daughter being curled up in a ball on the floor like a mushroom and having a tantrum, I decided to **join her in her activity** (page 69). I realised, from my "mushroom", that I wanted a hug! I snuck over to her mushroom and waited. As I sensed her calming down, I asked if I could have a hug, which we did. After that, everything was easier. It's great to get the insight that she needs the physical reassurance and attention of a hug. I did good.*

Result!

Take care of YOU

Sonia

I read Mr Mischief *with my son tonight before his bedtime. He read a page and I read a page. I resisted my urge to hurry him along and tell him to stop fidgeting about on my lap (Arrgh!). Instead, I made a conscious effort to be calm (page 145) and focused on his concentration and enjoyment of our activity. He quickly settled down and I genuinely enjoyed his reading.*

Result!

Sandra

I regularly buy myself flowers now to acknowledge and reward myself for all that I do well as a parent. I enjoy seeing them on the kitchen window sill and they remind me what a great job I'm doing.

Result!

Mel

I realised I deserved and wanted a day off from my family every month. It works well for all of us. I do whatever I like. This has so far included meeting up with friends (child-free!) and catching a movie. My most indulgent was a day at a health spa. Worth every penny!

Result!

Take care of YOU

You're doing great!

Stick with it!

Keep going!

Give yourself a good talking to

5

One day I took my two children out in the car to go for a walk in the country. It wasn't a very nice day but I reckoned we all needed some fresh air and a change of scene. We parked and my eldest was really up for the walk, getting out and putting her coat on. Meanwhile, my youngest refused to get out, adamant that she didn't want to go for a walk.

I was feeling increasingly "not OK", as this stern, parental voice inside my head was telling me

What a stupid idea, thinking you could drag her out on a day like today. You're really selfish forcing the kids out to do what you want to do, always thinking of yourself… Stupid, selfish… bad parent!

I was just about to turn that same tone of voice on my youngest child when I caught sight of myself in the rear view mirror. What a thunderous face! I gave myself an exasperated shrug and sigh. And in that moment, another calmer, kinder and supportive voice in my head started telling me

You're trying to do your best for your children. What a great idea you've had to change the scene and get some fresh air. You'll all feel better for some exercise and you know the kids will enjoy it once they get going. Stick with it… You're doing great!

With that voice in my head encouraging me, I was able to use a calm, persuasive voice with my younger daughter. My thinking was clearer, my mood was better and from then on I was "OK". We all enjoyed our walk.

Take care of YOU

That experience taught me to be more aware of the way I talked to myself and how this influenced my behaviour. I noticed that when I was talking to myself in a helpful, supportive way, my behaviour was correspondingly supportive and useful. So I explored how to be my own "best friend", how to develop a helpful, supportive voice to counter the critical, self-defeating inner voice that can sometimes take over. The following method will help you **give yourself a *good* talking to:**

The method

There are two stages. Stage 1 is about quietening the voice of your "Inner Critic". Stage 2 helps you to develop the voice of your own "Inner Best Friend".

Stage 1: Quieten your Inner Critic

When you notice that the way you are talking to yourself is negative, overly critical or self-defeating, then change the qualities of this unhelpful voice in order to reduce its impact. Notice:

- **the volume:** is it loud or quiet?
    Adjustment: Make it quieter

- **the tone and character:** is it harsh or soft, stern, mocking, sarcastic?
    Adjustment: Make it softer, kinder

- **the voice**: is it yours or someone else's?
    Adjustment: Make it a distinctive, amusing voice, e.g. Donald Duck, Homer Simpson, Dame Edna Everage

- **where it comes from:** is it inside or outside of you? Where specifically?
    Adjustment: Make it lower and more distant, e.g. move it from your shoulder or the front of your head to your big toe, or far away from you.

Here's an example:

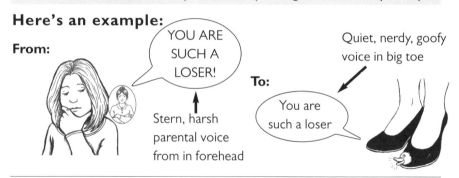

From:
YOU ARE SUCH A LOSER!
Stern, harsh parental voice from in forehead

To:
You are such a loser
Quiet, nerdy, goofy voice in big toe

Take care of YOU

Now that you have diminished your Inner Critic, let it speak again. Notice how it's hard now to take what it's saying seriously. If it still has an unpleasant impact on you, make some more adjustments, this time more extreme and comical.

Stage 2: Develop the voice of your Inner Best Friend
Think of a really kind, helpful and supportive voice; a voice you can trust to be calm, fair, objective and helpful. This can be the voice of a good friend or someone you admire, someone you know who sees the best in you or, indeed, your own calm voice. It needs to be different from your Inner Critic.

Close your eyes and imagine this voice talking to you. As you listen, notice:

- **the tone and character** of this voice.

- **where this voice is coming from.** Does it come from inside or outside of you? Where specifically?

- **how this voice makes you feel:** reassured, calmer, safer, more grounded, inspired, proud of yourself and your efforts, that you're doing your best.

- **any other associations** you have with this voice, such as images in your mind, memories or past experiences.

- **what this voice is saying to you**, the words it uses and the effect these words have on you.

Enjoy the presence of your Inner Best Friend and the effect it has on you. Know that by making this voice your focus of attention, you can listen to it any time you like. It is a resource that is always there for you.

Here's an example:

It's going to be OK. You're doing the best you can. Give yourself a break.

Practise quietening your Inner Critic and redirecting your attention to your Inner Best Friend.

Take care of YOU

Here's another example:

From:

You're late again getting the kids ready for school. You know they need 15 minutes to get ready… You've got 10 minutes left and you've only just told them. It's going to be a real pain to get them out the door and you're bound to forget something…

To:

Remember, when you're calm, they do things faster. Take a few deep breathes now… That's better. Let them do what they have to do. Notice their efforts and help them if they need it. Look calmly around… Check now that you've got everything ready that you need.

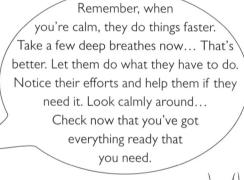

Late again

Tips for good results

✓ Reinforce the presence of your Inner Best Friend by including any image that come to mind: the face of the person whose voice you hear, or a situation from the past where this person really supported you. Make your Inner Best Friend part of your inner support team.

✓ Write down your findings about your Inner Best Friend to help you practise bringing them to mind and listening to their voice.

✓ The voice of your Inner Best Friend could be that of a person who is alive or dead, real or imagined, close or distant – whatever works best for you.

Take care of YOU

✓ Check out the **Practice makes permanent** method (page 209) to regularly hear the voice of your Inner Best Friend.

Now you have a go

Take some quiet time out to experiment with how you talk to yourself and how to develop your Inner Best Friend.

Stage 1: Quieten your Inner Critic

You can go straight to diminishing the voice of your actual Inner Critic or explore first with the voice of someone you really don't like. Imagine the voice saying something that makes you feel inadequate. Then make the voice quieter, kinder and comical. Now move it to a non-threatening location and allow it to speak again. You'll know if you've removed the power of this negative voice when its words no longer affect you emotionally.

Now, what would you like to hear instead?

Stage 2: Develop the voice of your Inner Best Friend

You can go straight to finding and developing your Inner Best Friend voice as described in the method, or you can explore first with the voice of a public figure you admire. Hear this person's voice saying kind, reassuring, encouraging, positive words you'd like to hear. Accept what it is saying and notice how you cannot help but smile.

Enjoy the warmth and support of this voice. As you listen to it, notice the characteristics of this voice and where it is coming from. You can make a note of these to make it easier to recall this voice in the future.

If you have explored Stage 2 using the voice of a public figure you admire, be sure to repeat this stage to develop the voice of your Inner Best Friend. Add this voice to your growing inner support team!

Take care of YOU

And finally...

In the modern world, you may feel bombarded by noise, especially the sound of voices. These voices and their messages come not only from people around you but also from the radio, TV, phones and computer technology in various forms. These voices can be unpleasant or pleasant, negative or positive, harmful or useful, discouraging or encouraging.

So be discerning. If you surround yourself with negative voices, it's easy to fall into a negative spiral of moaning and complaining, and much harder to think positively. Recognise how words and voices influence you. Choose who and what you want to listen to, inside your head and in the outside world!

How this method worked for...

Ali

When I used this method to develop my Inner Best Friend, I had this really strong image of a kind, supportive "big sister" coming and sitting next to me when I was upset as a child, sitting on the kerb of the pavement with my feet in the gutter. I'm sure she has a calm, reassuring voice, but to be honest, she doesn't say much – she just listens patiently as I tell her my woes. I find this image enduringly reassuring and invoke it when I feel like I need a hug! I also feel really reassured and proud of myself as a parent when I notice myself behaving in this "big sisterly" way with my own children.

Result!

Jane

Once I started to play around with my Inner Critic, I realised the impact that the TV was having on me. I used to habitually watch the soaps and the news before I went to bed. I now realise how negative and self-defeating the characters and voices generally are in the soaps. I also realise that the news is usually negative and unpleasant. No wonder I used to go to bed feeling miserable!

Now, I watch much less TV and am really picky about what I do watch. Instead of watching the news on TV, I keep up with what's going on online. It's great to take control of what's going into my head and I have more time now that I'm not stuck in front of the TV any more. My inner voice is much more positive and I'm much happier... And so are my kids – we've cut back on their viewing time and replaced TV with DVDs.

Result!

Find your good mood

In your role as a parent, do you often find yourself in a *less than good* mood, maybe feeing unhappy and frustrated, unduly stressed, anxious or depressed?

Having children affects people in different ways. Depending on our previous life experiences, we have different expectations of what family life will be like and what it will mean to us. Some of us have a sense of ourselves and our self-worth prior to having children that continues into family life. We find ways to combine our needs with the needs of our children and families. However, on becoming parents, some of us find it harder to maintain a sense of who we are in this stage of our lives, given the demands now being made upon us.

It was only after I had had my first child that I realised how much I'd previously been in control of my life, pretty much choosing what I wanted to do. I'd been at the centre of my world. Overnight, my world was taken over by this baby 24/7. I was effectively knocked off centre; I completely lost track of what my needs were, never mind how to meet them.

There is a danger that we simply get lost in the relentlessness of family life, unable to recognise or meet our own needs. Alternatively, we may feel trapped, spending all of our time, energy and money doing something that is rewarding up to a point, but it isn't enough. And this is the only job we can't resign from!

The extent to which you feel personally satisfied and fulfilled by being a parent depends on your individual expectations and preferences. There may be other aspects of your life that are equally or more important to you in terms of the level of enjoyment and personal satisfaction you gain from them. These could include your work, relationships, wider family and community, being creative, artistic or athletic, your interests and hobbies, your spirituality or religious practice.

Seeking to balance your needs in these areas into the mix of family life and your parenting commitments makes you a better parent because you're happier. Your good mood enables you to think and act more usefully towards your children. You're also better able to adjust your expectations in situations that used to frustrate you in family life because you know that there is more to you than just being a parent.

The following two methods give you ways to **balance your needs into the mix** and **adjust your expectations.**

 # Balance your needs into the mix

The method

To start to recognise and understand what your needs are, ask yourself:

What's important to me in life?

What do I enjoy?

What makes me feel worthwhile? ... satisfied? ... fulfilled?

Make a list, jotting down anything and everything that springs to mind. This list is personal to you; there are no right or wrong answers.

Compare and rank the items on your list in terms of their importance to you.

Now consider the extent to which you are currently doing what's important to you. How much of your time, energy and money do you currently spend pursuing the items on your list? Consider how the amount of time, energy and money you spend meeting the needs of your children and supporting family life compares with other items on your list:

Their needs 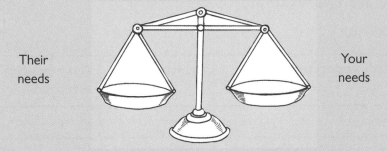 Your needs

Give yourself permission to **balance your needs into the mix**: to meet your needs *alongside* those of your family. You're worth it! Your family deserves and will benefit from it too: a happier, healthier you!

Identify steps you can take to use your time more wisely or creatively, to combine your needs more effectively into family life.

Tips for good results

✓ Perhaps at the moment, you can only take *small steps* towards doing what's important for you. This is a way of maintaining contact with those other parts of your life, which, in due course, as circumstances change, will have a bigger part to play once more.

✓ The way you achieve balance in your life will be unique to you. If you find yourself making comparisons with others, resist the urge to feel guilty or make judgements. Instead stay open and curious about how others achieve what works for them. Be willing to copy anything that you think will serve you – and then make it your own. (**It's cool to copy!** page 193, explores how to learn by copying your children and can be applied equally well to "grown ups".)

✓ **Balancing your needs into the mix** is an ongoing process. What's important to you, the needs of your family and your circumstances will undoubtedly change over time. So make this method a regular review of how you are meeting your needs, alongside those of your family, to **find your good mood**.

Here are two examples:

Example 1

What's important to me:	Ranking	Am I meeting this need?
Family	1 equal	✓
Work – supporting my family	1 equal	✓
Exercise – running/swimming	3	✗
Healthy eating	5	sometimes!
A social life…	4	✗

Take care of YOU

Steps towards a better balance:

I want to get fitter and healthier again: I'm currently overweight, unfit and feel like a slob. I want to get some exercise, any exercise, whenever I can. So I need to:

- *take my running kit to work so I can take a lunchtime jog if time allows – be prepared!*
- *arrange childcare so that I can swim at our local pool one evening a week.*

I also want to eat more healthily, which means I need to:

- *get more fruit in … and eat it! I can do this straight away.*
- *meal plan, write a shopping list and use it! This will take more effort and discipline.*

Example 2

What's important to me:	Ranking	Am I meeting this need?
Family	I equal	✓
A social life – "out there" with adults!	I equal	✗
Friends – I just don't see them any more	3	✗
Healthy eating	4	mostly
Crafts – making things	5	with the kids
Work	6	✗

Steps towards a better balance:

I need a break – some "me" time; a chance to catch up with a friend …I really need to:

- *arrange some childcare so I can do this.*
- *make the effort to ring my friends in the evening, once the kids are asleep.*

I can then start thinking about how to build up my confidence to get back into some kind of work…

Take care of YOU

Now you have a go

Take some calm time to work through the steps of this method. Make sure you start by exploring what's important to you. Be completely honest. Writing a list of what's important to you sets your creative unconscious mind to work on coming up with ideas as to how you may be able to pursue these things. Simply recognising what is important to you is the first step in an ongoing process towards better balance.

Notice the reality of your current situation by considering how much of your time and energy you spend on what's important to you compared to meeting the needs of your children and family. This isn't meant to make you feel guilty or inadequate about your current situation. It is intended to be an opportunity for you to start to find ways to use your time more wisely. And it may not be obvious yet how you will be able to make progress towards achieving what's important to you.

You can have some fun with this method by going through it with a sympathetic friend or partner. Do some plotting, scheming and dreaming! This is also a great way to take some enjoyable, relaxing "you" time with a friend: a reward for all your ongoing efforts to support your children and family. **Be impressed** with each other and **celebrate your successes** (page 159).

And finally ...

There are many books dedicated to time management and achieving life balance. **Balance your needs into the mix** simply helps you to recognise the importance of meeting your needs to **find your good mood**, for your benefit and that of your family.

Find ways, however small, to bring what's important to you into the ongoing mix of family life. Like adding a pinch of salt to a recipe, it's amazing the difference you can make by spending just a little time doing something that's really important to you.

Take care of YOU

How this method worked for ...

Jane

I love listening and dancing to loud music – I used to "just do it" before we had children. When I worked through this method, I realised that I hadn't done it in years... So I dug out my music and "just did it" again! Wow, what a buzz! I feel great and the kids join in too. We all play air guitar together!

Result!

Roz

I was interested in exploring my needs because I've had this growing sense of "pouring cold water onto my brain" every day, caring for my young children, fulltime. Before we had children, I was a successful professional artist. This method helped me acknowledge just how important my creativity is to me.

My first small step was simply having a sketchbook on the work surface in the kitchen so that I could jot down any ideas as they came to me. A small step but allowing my ideas to flow again made me feel more alive and enthusiastic. It is this enthusiasm that I believe has somehow drawn clients back to me and enabled me to negotiate commissions that work around my family.

Result!

Take care of YOU

Take care of *YOU*

Adjust your expectations

The method

When you are at your wits' end with a specific situation or feeling generally frustrated with your current circumstances, ask yourself:

What expectations do I currently have of myself and others?

Consider for a moment what it would be like to let go of those expectations. What other possibilities are you now aware of that would be more personally fulfilling for you in your current circumstances? Ask yourself:

What expectations would make life easier: kinder on me and others?

Accept that you can adjust your expectations in your current circumstances in order to make your life easier and be kinder to yourself and others.

Here's an example:

Situation:
I'm really frustrated by the untidy state of our house with clothes, toys, stuff everywhere. I hate the way that I can't seem to get on top of it any more.

What expectations do I currently have of myself and others?
I want to make the house clear and tidy like I used to be able to.

Letting go of these expectations, I am aware that:
Now we have children, the tidying up, cleaning up, washing and sorting out are never-ending. There never comes a time when everything is finished. This is what life is like with more of us living in this space.

What expectations would make life easier: kinder on me and others?
It's unrealistic to expect myself to make the house look the way it used to. Now that we have children, all this stuff is actually a sign of life happening in this space. So:

- *I could enjoy the odd moments when things look tidier? No, that doesn't really work.*

- *I know: I can make sure that the lounge is tidy and clutter free at the end of every day. This can be "my tidy space". From now on, I will no longer feel solely responsible for making everywhere else clear and tidy. Instead, I will think of these other spaces as our collective responsibility as a family to make clear and tidy.*

Tips for good results

✓ This method is great for helping you feel better in your current circumstances about a situation that you can't change. What you can do is choose to change your attitude.

✓ This method is similar to **Find a useful meaning** (page 103), which helps you to change the way you look at what your child is doing. This method helps you change the way you look at what you are doing so that you can feel more comfortable about it and get on with it more easily.

✓ Give yourself a pat on the back when you successfully use this method. You have overcome your immediate response, found a different, more effective response and got a good result. Well done! (**Be impressed ... with you!** page 153, has further ideas on giving yourself effective praise.)

Take care of YOU

Now you have a go

Think of a situation recently where you felt compromised in meeting your needs. With this situation in mind, ask yourself:

What expectations did I have of myself and others?

As you reflect on this situation, allow yourself to realise how your expectations constrained you and what it could have been like without these expectations. Ask yourself:

What expectations would have made life easier: kinder on me and others?

Smile as you notice how else you could have interpreted this situation and how much easier it would have been for you if this had been your focus. Accept that you now have more realistic expectations that will make life easier and will be kinder on you and others in future situations.

And finally ...

There are times in life when things are not the way you would like them to be. Recognising and pursuing what's important to you in life is a great way to be in a good mood more of the time. This was explored in the first method, **Balance your needs into the mix**.

Adjust your expectations is for those times when you're acutely aware of the fact that you can't do what you love. In those circumstances, change your attitude and, for the moment, love what you do.

Take care of YOU

How this method worked for ...

Ellen

I was getting really frustrated with being a housewife, washing, cooking, cleaning ... I didn't value what I was doing because it was so mindless and monotonous and yet I thought I was supposed to feel fulfilled by it. For me, the term "housewife" meant mindless, bland and dull – like a "Stepford Wife".

By letting go of my expectations about what a housewife is, I realised that, though monotonous, housework is vital to the health and happiness of my family and a smooth running family life. So I stopped thinking of myself as a housewife and now think of housework as "family support work".

It's made a big difference! Because I've "professionalised" my family support work, I go about it much more efficiently. Instead of thinking I need to find my personal fulfilment in this work, I get it done as quickly as possible so that I can get on with things I do find more interesting and personally fulfilling.

Result!

Sam

I used to get a real buzz out of exercise, feeling fit, healthy and in control. I realised that, after we had children, I'd stopped doing any because I felt I couldn't do it "properly" any more, meaning I couldn't commit to a schedule, enter events, improve my performance, etc. So I adjusted my expectations and let go of "doing it properly". Instead, I gave myself permission to just do it whenever I got the chance.

I'm really surprised at how significant this change in attitude has been for me. Now, I simply love getting exercise whenever I can. I think it gives me even more of a buzz because I'm much more flexible and open to opportunities as they arise.

Result!

Take care of YOU

Section 4

Enjoy the journey

Learning from and with your children

Introduction

So far the methods in this book have looked at ways of responding more usefully in situations involving you and your children through what you say, do, think and the mood you're in. The methods in this section give you the opportunity to take a step back from the challenges of family life to look at the learning opportunities that your children present you with. It's obvious to think of your children as learners, learning from you, the "grown up". It's perhaps less obvious, but no less significant, to realise how much you can learn from your children that will help you on your learning journey as a parent.

Young children are natural learners. They embody learning through experience; they just get on and have a go. Isn't it inspiring watching your children programme and re-programme themselves towards the result they want in front of your very eyes? And over a period of a few months, look at what children achieve:

From sitting to crawling, to walking and talking, every experience is an *in the moment* learning adventure for a young child.

The first two methods show you how to learn from your children. Watch them, listen to them and appreciate their insights into life, the world we live in and what they can tell you about yourself!

These methods are:

- Walk your talk
- It's cool to copy!

The two methods that follow give you ways to *build on what works* supporting your learning journey as you try new approaches, explore different perspectives and get different results. These methods help you extend your "toolkit" of **Happy Kids Happy You** techniques, so that you get the most out of them and have a family life that works for you.

They are:

- How was it for you?
- Practice makes permanent.

Moments of choice concludes this section. It brings together all the methods in this book and reminds you of those moments, those **pauses for thought**, when you realise you can choose a different approach.

Walk your talk

This method explores what we can learn from our children when they draw attention to our undesirable behaviour. They can bring inconsistencies in what we say and do into sharp focus in a number of ways:

- They copy our undesirable behaviour from us:

> *Children are natural mimics; they act like their parents*
> *in spite of every effort to teach them good manners.*
>
> Anonymous

- They *want* to copy our undesirable behaviour from us. For example,

Once we'd had our children and I'd come to the end of five years of being pregnant and breastfeeding, my eating habits had completely gone to pot. I was in "see it, eat it" mode, regardless of whether I was hungry or not. I found myself eating all sorts of stuff, food I didn't even like, such as the kids' leftover marmite on toast – yuk! Whilst I provided healthy food for the kids and only allowed them fruit at snack times, I frequently "found myself" sneaking biscuits from the cupboard when I didn't think they were looking. One day, my 3-year-old caught me unawares, mid-munch, and said "Mummy, I want a biscuit too!"

- They simply give us honest feedback about how we are behaving, such as

"Mummy, you need to calm down!" or *"Please don't use your cross voice."*

However they do it, whenever your children make you aware of inconsistencies in what you're saying or doing, they present you with an opportunity to change your ways. Bringing your own behaviour into line with what you want for your children has the following benefits:

- Your new behaviour gets better results for you.

- You're demonstrating behaviour that you'd be happy for your children to copy from you.

- You're also demonstrating continuing personal development for your children: the ability to learn at any age and change what you are doing to something more beneficial.

Enjoy the journey

HAPPY KIDS HAPPY YOU **185**

Here's a method to help you reap these benefits and **walk your talk**:

The method

When you find yourself wanting one thing for your child but doing something else yourself, ask yourself:

- **Why is it important for my child to behave in the way that I want them to?**
- **What benefits does this behaviour get for them?**

When you've identified the benefits for your child, consider:

> *If I want these benefits for my children, I deserve them for myself.*

Recognise that you can have the same benefits by behaving consistently with what you want your child to do. You will also be consistently demonstrating that behaviour to your child.

Once you are convinced that you want these benefits, ask yourself:

- **What now needs to happen for me to *walk my talk*?**
- **What do I need to do differently?**
- **How will I support myself through these changes?**
- **How will this work for me *and* for my child?**

Now that you have identified what you need to do, are these things that you can and will do? If so, decide when and how you will put them into practice. If not, ask yourself the above questions again and focus on how **walking your talk** will work for you as well as your child.

Be impressed with yourself as you do something different and make changes. Well done! Also be impressed with yourself and your child when you notice that your child's behaviour has changed too. (See pages 51 and 153 for more on how to **be impressed** with your children and yourself respectively.)

Here's an example: "From biscuits to apples"

When my 3-year-old caught me secretively eating biscuits from the cupboard, I realised that, if I wanted my children to eat healthily, I had to take a look at my own eating habits.

Why is it important for my child to behave in the way that I want them to? What benefits does this behaviour get for them?

- *When my kids just have fruit between meals, they eat well at mealtimes.*
- *They're learning the difference between food their bodies need, a healthy balanced diet, and treats like sweets, desserts, biscuits, etc.*
- *They're healthy, happy and enjoy fruit. It's good for their teeth too.*

If I want these benefits for my children, I deserve them for myself.

I deserve to eat healthily too! If I follow the same eating habits as my kids, I'll look and feel a whole lot better. I could lose the weight I've put on through having babies and breastfeeding. Then I could wear all my nice clothes again.

What now needs to happen for me to *walk my talk*?

I need to get rid of the biscuits. My kids don't need them and neither do I!

What do I need to do differently?

I need to buy more fruit and eat it when my kids do. I can still enjoy occasional treats but I need to learn more regular, healthy eating habits.

How will I support myself through these changes?

I will write down what I'm eating to get more conscious control of the food that goes in my mouth. I'll be impressed with my efforts and get my friend to support me. We can encourage each other as I know she wants to lose weight too.

How will this work for me and for my child?

I can be open about what I'm eating instead of trying to sneak biscuits. I can be impressed with my kids' good eating habits and get them to encourage me to eat like them!

Be impressed with yourself and your child as you do something different and make changes. Well done!

Stopped eating kids' marmite on toast – hurrah! I actually quite like apples. Yesterday, I was about to cut an apple up for my 3-year-old when she said, "I want a whole apple, like you Mummy!"
Result!

Enjoy the journey

Tips for good results

✓ Of course, there are times when it's entirely appropriate for you to behave differently to your child. This could be because your adult behaviour – such as using a mobile phone – simply isn't relevant to your child. This won't stop your child wanting to copy you, so simply redirect them, using a method such as **Turn Don'ts into Do's** (page 27).

Also take into account the difference between how adults and children behave in meeting the same need, e.g. different bedtimes or meal portion sizes. It's usually quite straightforward to explain these distinctions in behaviour to your child, as required.

✓ Be aware that there are other influences on your child. You may find yourself thinking, "Where did they learn *that?*" When you know they didn't get it from you, use methods such as **Turn Don't into Do's** (page 27), **Turn Stop's into Go's** (page 33) or **Set and maintain reasonable boundaries** (page 89) to encourage and support the behaviours you do want.

✓ This method offers you an opportunity to think about the kind of role model you are for your child. In doing so, you may well find yourself thinking about what's important to you and how you currently honour your needs and wants. **Find your good mood** (page 169) helps you explore what's important to you so that you can take good care of yourself.

Now you have a go

The key to this method is acknowledging that undesirable behaviours are not the sole domain of children; you demonstrate them too! Being open to the possibility that *you* could be contributing to or even creating challenging situations with your children gives you the opportunity to change yourself for the better. You can become more self-aware, supporting and encouraging your own learning and personal development.

When you identify one of your own undesirable behaviours, you may feel surprised, annoyed, embarrassed, ashamed or guilty. You may feel reluctant to admit your undesirable behaviour to yourself or anyone else. So be kind to yourself, recognise that no one is perfect, that to err is human. The good news is that once you *know* your behaviour is undesirable, you can do something about it.

Work through this method to identify the benefits you can gain and the changes you want to make. At first, you may not know what needs to happen to **walk your talk**. Some changes may be quite simple and straightforward; other situations may require more wide reaching changes in your attitude, thinking and habits. Stay focused on the benefits you can gain for yourself and your children. Take the time you need to decide how you want to pursue these benefits.

Doing something different can be uncomfortable at first as you move beyond your current comfort zone. This is a positive sign that you're learning something new so stick with it. **Practice makes permanent** (page 209) has more on supporting yourself making changes.

Make sure you seek any help and support you need from others. This could be the cooperation of your children or partner, the support of a friend or help from teachers, trainers, coaches or other service providers in the field of personal change. There are always people out there who can help you and there are also many books on personal development and change. (The **References and further reading** in **Appendix III** has some suggestions.)

Enjoy the journey

And finally...

It can be quite daunting, thinking about what kind of role model you are for your children and wondering if they will pick up all your faults. Better to think of yourself as a role model for life-long learning, demonstrating to your children that nobody is perfect and that adults also adapt, learn and change.

Recognise the learning opportunity your children give you when they draw attention to your undesirable behaviours. Learn alongside them for their benefit and yours.

How this method worked for...

Phil

My daughter appeared to have acquired an annoying habit of requesting things by pointing at them and grunting their name, such as pointing at her drink and grunting, "Drink!" At first I ignored this, not wanting to reinforce it by drawing attention to it. However, this behaviour persisted and became more frequent. One morning, as we were leaving the house, I noticed myself pointing at her shoes and saying, "Shoes!" as my short-hand for "Please put your shoes on." Next moment, there I was saying, "Coat!" and pointing at her coat, to mean, "Please put your coat on."

When I thought about it, I realised that I had developed and demonstrated this behaviour in my hurry to get us out of the door in the mornings. My daughter was simply copying my impolite behaviour! Once I stopped doing it and more consistently asked her to do things politely, in a gentler tone, she appeared to follow my lead and the "point and grunt" died away.

Result!

Tina

As my first child became more independent with her eating, I found myself wanting her to quickly eat everything I gave her. I became impatient and forceful with her, saying I was "giving" her time to eat but the next moment fussing over her and interfering, not really giving her time at all. I recognised that my behaviour mirrored how my grandmother had behaved towards me as a child, which made me feel really uncomfortable. I didn't really want to face up to my overbearing behaviour, but I knew I wanted to do something about it.

When I considered my own eating behaviour, I realised I rushed to eat my food and

Enjoy the journey

didn't take time to enjoy it. This was because I was usually busy thinking about everything else that I needed to do. My upbringing also compelled me to eat everything on my plate, even if I was already full. I realised I wanted to give myself more time to relax and enjoy my food in order to feel more relaxed about my child taking the time she needed to feed herself and enjoy her food.

I still find it hard to take time to enjoy eating, but I now make a conscious effort to eat more slowly. I'm better at recognising when I'm full and perhaps leaving some food on my plate. This has helped me accept that it's OK for my child to leave food too. I'm also better at recognising when she is actually eating and I can leave her to get on with it.

Result!

Enjoy the journey

It's cool to copy!

15⁺

I first realised I could learn something really useful by *copying my child* when she was about 18 months old:

> From 18 months onwards, she started to challenge me, finding and testing boundaries. She could be in the throes of a major tantrum one moment, totally committed to wailing and thrashing. Yet the next moment, she could be happy and laughing. Having risen to her challenge and the intensity of her tantrum, I would then be left cross and annoyed, in a bad mood, whilst she simply "switched" to being OK again. Sometimes my bad mood stayed with me for the rest of the day, a kind of "emotional hangover" from the morning battles.
>
> I became jealous and resentful of her ability to "switch" her mood, until one day it occurred to me that I was really rather impressed by her switch-ability. Here I was, holding on to my bad mood, while she could simply let go and move on. How did she do that?! It dawned on me that perhaps I could copy her and learn to let go and move on too...

Recognising and copying abilities and qualities that you admire in your child has the following benefits:

- It's a great way to compliment and be impressed with your child. They get your recognition and appreciation as you pay particular attention to their positive qualities and abilities.

- It's a "licence to explore" with your child: you get to find out more about *their world* and what works for them; you can be curious about their insights and interests.

- It acknowledges that copying and learning can work both ways between you and your child. This nurtures respect, trust and a sense of being on an equal footing in your relationship with them.

- It's a **win-win** situation, as there's something in it for both you and your child.

Enjoy the journey

Copying is a natural learning process for human beings. We all did it as children and still do it now, to a greater or lesser extent, whether we are consciously aware of it or not. The following method suggests ways that you can more deliberately copy and acquire the abilities that you admire in your children.

The method

Identify the ability you would like to copy by asking yourself:

- **What really impresses me about my child?**
- **Is this something that I would like to be able to do too?**

This could be something that amazes and challenges you, because you have no idea how they do it!

Recognise and build on any skills you already have in this area, even those which are just a little bit in that direction. Think creatively and you're bound to find something there. Ask yourself:

- **To what extent do I already do this? When and where?**

To identify situations where this ability would benefit you, ask yourself:

- **When and where do I want to be able to do this?**
- **What results could I achieve through having this ability?**

Now get really familiar with your child's ability. Find out as much as you can by watching, listening and "tuning in" to your child as they demonstrate this ability. You can also:

- Match them (page 75). This gives you information about their body language and also about their mood.

- **Join them in their activity** (page 69). This gives you information about what they are doing and how they do it.

- Take some calm time out to **find out what your body knows** about your child's ability (page 125). Get an understanding of what your child is thinking and their intentions as they do what they do.

Enjoy the journey

Now you are ready to try out your version of your child's ability. Notice the results you get as you try something different. Practise and fine-tune your ability until you get the results you want.

Be impressed … with you! (page 153) as you try out something new and different with the aim of getting a better result.

Here are two examples:

Example 1: "Let go and move on"

What really impresses me about my child?

She can "switch" her mood from angry to happy in an instant.

Is this something that I would like to be able to do too?

*Yes! I want to be able to **let go and move on…** just like that!*

To what extent do I already do this? When and where?

Not sure. I guess my mood changes after I've dropped the kids at nursery and head off to work.

When and where do I want to be able to do this?

After my child has challenged me, testing boundaries and throwing tantrums. She just "switches" and moves on… but I don't!

What results could I achieve through having this ability?

I could move on from my child's mood changes more easily. I wouldn't feel resentful towards my child. I could feel refreshed, like an "emotional reset". I could be in a better mood for the rest of the day.

Get really familiar with your child's ability. Find out as much as you can by watching, listening and "tuning in" to your child as they demonstrate this ability.

*When she "switches" she completely changes her focus of attention: she's totally distracted and absorbed by something else. I use **Turn Don'ts into Do's** (page 27) to distract her in this way….*

Aha! So I need to try completely distracting myself and totally replacing my negative emotions with something else ... This needs to be something I really love about life – music, dancing, happy memories of when I felt great... Yes, I feel great already!

In doing this, I need to let go of my negative emotions so that I don't come back to them later. Knowing that I don't need them may help me do this – they don't serve any useful purpose and only make me miserable.

Try out your version of your child's ability. Notice the results you get as you try something different. Practise and fine-tune your ability until you get the results you want.

I've tried this and it works: putting on lively music or remembering how great I felt on our summer holiday enable me to switch my mood completely. I know I always have a choice now: to hold on to my "bad mood" or to completely distract myself.

Be impressed ... with you! (page 153) as you try out something new and different.

I can manage my mood better. I'm happier and life's easier – hurrah!

Example 2: "Have a go!"

What really impresses me about my child?

They just get right on in there and have a go! They have no fear! They're also supremely persistent: when their efforts don't get the results they seek, they simply have another go ... and another ... and another. Giving up is not an option!

Is this something that I would like to be able to do too? *Yes!*

To what extent do I already do this? When and where?

*I guess becoming a parent has really stretched me to **have a go** at things I wouldn't have done before, like singing to them (!), complaining in restaurants about bad food or service. I do these things for my kids' sake. It would be great to do them for my own sake ...*

When and where do I want to be able to do this?

I'd love to be able to sing confidently and make a joyous, tuneful noise... I'd also love to be able to stand up for myself in the way that I stand up for my kids.

Enjoy the journey

What results could I achieve through having this ability?

I would feel more confident and value myself and my abilities. I would be brave for my own sake. I guess I also want to role model these qualities for my kids as they grow up…

Get really familiar with your child's ability. Find out as much as you can by watching, listening and "tuning in" to your child as they demonstrate this ability.

My youngest child has no fear and has not yet developed much common sense. I make situations safe for her. She is completely open to experiencing a situation because she hasn't learned to analyse or make judgements yet.

*Aha! I need to make new experiences "safe enough" for me to **have a go**. I also need to hold off analysing and thinking too much.*

She seems to be driven by her enthusiasm and excitement for everything that is new to her… which is most things!

*Aha! When I feel driven by excitement and enthusiasm about something new, I feel fear too … So I can think of this tingly, butterflies in my stomach kind of fear as actually being a good indicator that this is something I really want to **have a go** at…*

Try out your version of your child's ability. Notice the results you get as you try something different. Practise and fine-tune your ability until you get the results you want.

*I'm enjoying learning new things again, "putting myself out there" more in order to **have a go**. I'm making it "safe enough" for me to do this by using **Practice makes permanent** (page 209) and **How was it for you?** (page 201) to support my learning experiences.*

I decided to take some singing lessons so I could be more confident about my singing voice. I recently led some singing with a group of people. What a buzz! By recognising my tingly fear as the inseparable twin of my excitement, I was able to really enjoy this new experience.

Be impressed … with you! (page 153) as you try out something new and different.

I'm really proud that I can now enjoying singing in public and also encourage others to enjoy singing as a result of being inspired by and copying my child!

Tips for good results:

✓ Remember that you'll be developing *your version* of your child's ability. You cannot be your child! Adopt the bits that are relevant and work for you as you emulate their ability.

✓ Enjoy the interests and hobbies that your child introduces you to. Do these together if they are of interest to you too!

✓ Be *inspired* by your children! What do you notice that impresses you and that you'd like to emulate? Here are a few more suggestions.

Young children are:

- **refreshingly direct!** They simply "tell it how it is" from their point of view. They also have fewer social inhibitions with each other and just get on with talking and playing together.

- **insatiably curious!** They embody *wonder* at the world. Jump on this bandwagon and get curious again. Find out about stuff you've always wondered about.

- **opportunists!** They'll give anything a go just to see what happens!

- **imaginative!** They can role play and explore the world as someone else. They are flexible and creative in finding solutions and novel ways forward.

More about copying:

✓ Learning by copying is a great way to promote a **win-win** attitude. The person who excels in an ability gets the benefits of having the ability and being admired for it; the other person has someone they can copy and learn from.

As children get a bit older, they start to compare themselves with other children. Instead of the **lose** position of feeling jealous and belittled by the abilities of others, you can encourage your child to "become a detective" and find out how others do what they do. Support your child observing and copying the abilities of others. Your child then has the choice to develop their abilities as they wish to.

Enjoy the journey

✓ Who are your role models? What qualities and abilities do they embody that you would like? Copying others who have abilities and qualities you admire is not restricted to your children. You can use this method to find out more about how anybody you admire does what they do. (There's more on "clever copying" in Appendix II).

And finally...

There are undoubtedly situations where it's not **cool to copy**: for example, during school tests. That said, copying is an essential part of how we learn from each other. So let's reap the benefits of this powerful learning process and value it alongside our abilities to think, analyse and make sense of things.

How this method worked for...

Patrick

I love the way my young children live so completely in "the now". Whether they are exploring the texture of sand or away in a world of make-believe, they are completely absorbed in the present moment. **Concentrate on something mundane** *(page 147) and seeing how fulfilled my children are in "the now" has helped me calm down.*

Instead of stressing over what's happened or what's going to happen, I now take time to find fulfilment in the present moment. I also find the texture of sand fascinating, and the warmth of the sun on my face, and the sound of beautiful music, and the sight of a big full moon low on the horizon. My children are teaching me joyfulness.
Result!

Sally

I have always been fascinated by the piano and would love to be able to play but have always felt "too old" to start. However, when my daughter started lessons, I so enjoyed watching her learn that I started to copy her after she had finished. Soon, I was asking her to show me what she was playing and teach me to do it too.

This worked out really well: she could see me making mistakes as I learned which made her feel less conscious of her own mistakes. She felt proud to be able to show me something and I got to learn an instrument I had been drawn to for years. Now we sit together picking out tunes we have heard and really enjoy playing together and encouraging each other.
Result!

Enjoy the journey

Tony

Allowing myself to copy and learn from my children means I don't need "to have all the answers" any more. I no longer feel that I always need to be "the authority" and can enjoy learning alongside them. What a relief.

Result!

How was it for you?

20

This method provides a structure to help you reflect on your experiences if you find yourself feeling stuck, confused or stewing over a situation.

That was fantastic!

Gosh! That was rubbish… I did a really bad job…

Now I don't know what to think. I'm really confused…

There are lots of ways we naturally react to situations and experiences that enable us to process and reflect on things in order to reach a better understanding. For example, we may:

- chew things over
- meet, phone or text friends
- take a break
- get a change of scenery
- sleep on it
- get some exercise
- have a good night out
- rant and rage for a while
- weep
- see the funny side …

Any of these may help us to clear our heads, giving us new perspectives and understanding so that we can move on.

Sometimes though, when we're stewing or stuck, it's useful to have a more structured and purposeful way of working things through.

How was it for you gives you a way to process and reflect on your experiences. It offers four different perspectives that help you acknowledge your feelings and expand your thinking. As your head clears, you reach an understanding that allows you to move on, learning whatever you may need to learn on the way.

The method

The following questions help you to open up and explore four different perspectives on a situation or experience:

Fear
What was I afraid of?
What am I now afraid of?
What happened that scared me?

Frustration
What frustrated me?
What bored me?
What didn't I pay attention to?

Comfort
What went well?
What did I enjoy?
What can I celebrate?
What can I take comfort from specifically in this situation?
What can I take comfort from more generally?

Change
What did I learn?
What can I now learn?
What do I want for the future?
What will I do differently in the future?

There are two ways you can most usefully explore these questions:

Mark out these four perspectives on a sheet of paper, as shown below. Jot down your thoughts and ideas in each area as you consider the appropriate questions.

Fear	Frustration
Comfort	Change

Alternatively, you can process on the move:

Mark out a square on the floor using pieces of paper to label each corner with a different perspective, as shown below. Make the square as big as you can, given the space you have available. Go to each space in turn to consider the relevant questions for that area. Feel free to move around the spaces as your instincts guide you.

Fear	Frustration
Comfort	Change

When you are reflecting:

- Start with whichever aspect of your experience appeals to you first.

- Follow your instincts as to which area you go to next. You may find that your reflections regarding **Fear** and **Frustration** lead you to identify points for personal learning and development so go to the **Change** box and record these there.

- Make sure that, one way or another, you consider all four perspectives.

- Stop when you're ready. You'll know when you've reached an understanding that works for you.

- Record any actions or learning points that you want to follow up on.

Here's an example

The situation

We have had a really busy weekend. Lots going on: grandparents staying, ferrying kids to their activities, etc... Everything went well but I don't feel good; I feel overwhelmed, stressed and I'm worrying about stuff...

Fear	Frustration
What was I afraid of? What am I now afraid of? What happened that scared me? - *The behaviour of my youngest really scared me – the power of her tantrum... Afraid that I won't be able to cope...* - *Scared by my own frustration at not being able to keep on top of things...*	What frustrated me? What bored me? What didn't I pay attention to? - *Ate out on Saturday lunchtime and was stressed all the time – didn't enjoy it.* - *Got hooked into conflict situation with my youngest when I know it doesn't help either of us.* - *Ignored my own needs when I knew I needed some "time out". I could have easily had some...*
Comfort	**Change**
What went well? What did I enjoy? What can I celebrate or feel good about? What can I take comfort from ? - *Lovely to see kids with grandparents. All get on well.* - *Great Sunday lunch.* - *Kids doing really well in their activities. I got them there despite their reluctance!* - *Had a lovely walk with my eldest – some really nice quality time* - *Everything's going to be OK...*	What can I learn? What will I do differently in the future? - *Take care of **me**: listen to my inner voice; get some "me" time: e.g. exercise, a relaxing bath...* - *Realise that I always **do** cope one way or another. Realising this makes it easier for me to choose how to cope more effectively.*

Enjoy the journey

Follow up:
I'm going to have a relaxing bath now. Plan "me" time into the coming week. I'm only as good as my mood! Get some exercise; plan healthy meals for the week – I need and enjoy them too!

Tips for good results

✓ As you reflect on an experience you will find that your thinking and emotions change rapidly. Keep pace with whatever you're currently thinking or feeling by moving to the corresponding area and then ask yourself the associated questions. This helps you to unravel and separate out your thoughts and feelings into the four distinct areas. For example, if you're feeling scared, acknowledge this as fear and go to the **Fear** space. Consider the associated questions and acknowledge your fear. Then move into the **Comfort** area and ask yourself the associated questions. Make sure you leave all your fear in the **Fear** space and now allow yourself to feel comforted.

✓ Check out **Find a useful meaning** (page 103) for ways to explore what else a situation might mean.

✓ Perhaps the most important thing with this method is to get started! Even if you then have to break off to do something else, your unconscious will continue to process the questions. You can then come back to the structure of the method as you need to.

Now you have a go

To practise using this method, recall an experience you'd like to understand better. It could be a time you were particularly successful, enjoyed yourself, overcame your fears... anything at all! Whatever comes to mind first, go with it.

Have a go at exploring on the move. Put out four pieces of paper marked **Fear**, **Frustration**, **Comfort** and **Change**, at the corners of a square as shown in the method section above. As you move to each area ask yourself the relevant questions.

Keep pace with your thinking and feelings by moving to the next area that you need to deal with. Notice the different perspectives you get on the experience from the points of view of **Fear**, **Frustration**, **Comfort** and **Change**.

When you've explored enough, jot down any actions or learning points that you want to follow up.

Getting the hang of this method in this way means that you are more likely to think of using it and feel confident enough to have a go when you find yourself stuck or stewing.

And finally...

Our unconscious has an uncanny way of holding on to and reminding us of experiences that we still need to reflect on and process in some way. Use this method to open up your thinking and gain whatever learning you need to clear your head and move on.

How this method worked for...

Jayne

I was getting **frustrated** with my 4-year-old son being really clingy when I took him anywhere. He just wouldn't let go of me. Then I'd get upset too. My **fear** was that he somehow got the behaviour from me; that I was doing something wrong. It was all my fault.

I visited the **Frustration** and **Fear** spaces first and acknowledged my thoughts and feelings. Then I visited the **Comfort** space. Here, I could see that he was fine after I'd gone. He was also fine when the childminder dropped him off at activities. I could also see that he's a lovely, polite, happy boy and that other people have "clingy" children too!

Moving to the **Change** space, I could see that he only does this behaviour for me: I could think of it as all being a show for me! Seeing it like this, I could take comfort from the fact that he's fine after I've gone. This has helped me be calmer in the situation – or at least act it! I can now be more objectively sympathetic for him, without it becoming my problem too!

I felt much better having come to a calmer understanding of the situation and to have new ways of thinking about and dealing with it.

Result!

Jo

My two boys (aged 3 and 5) both got handheld computer learning systems for Christmas. At first, they weren't particularly interested in these but now I'm concerned about how much they want to play with them and how rude they can be when it's time to switch them off. I used this method because I felt confused and unclear about what to do. In exploring the four spaces, I gained clarity in my thinking and realised a few things as follows.

Comfort: I'm glad they enjoy using these systems. I'm comfortable that the content of the "games" they're playing are educational and that they're gaining early experience and skills in using computers in our technological age.

Fear: I'm afraid that their use of these systems is getting out of control. It's what they want to do all the time: they don't want to play out any more and it's increasingly hard to interest them in anything else. Their behaviour is becoming more aggressive. I'm worried they're interacting and communicating less with people. Where's this leading us?

Frustration: I feel guilty about the calm time I get when they're using these systems. The systems seem to have more power over them than I do and I don't really know what

Enjoy the journey

they're doing. Apparently, there's a facility to monitor what they're doing via the internet but I don't know how to work it and it feels like spying.

Change: *I'm surprised to realise the extent of my fears. It's good to gain some clarity and put my fears into a bigger picture. I can make some changes so that I'm more comfortable with how my children are using these systems.*

*I'll start by **joining them in their activity** (page 69) to find out more about what they're doing on these systems. This will make it easier for me to appreciate where they're up to and when would be a good time for them to stop. I can then use the **Set and maintain reasonable boundaries** method (page 89) to put clear boundaries in place to regulate their use of these systems, as necessary.*
Result!

Practice makes permanent

Knowledge is of no value unless you put it into practice.

Anton Chekhov

Practice is the best of all instructors.

Publilius Syrus

Practice puts brains in your muscles.

Sam Snead

With time and practice, the **Happy Kids Happy You** methods become *your way* of thinking and approaching situations. To the extent that you have tried these methods and experienced some different results, well done for moving out of your old comfort zone with the aim of getting better results for you and your children.

Opinions vary as to how many times or how long you have to practise something before it becomes *your way* – anything up to 180 times for a new muscle memory to stick in the brain. But one thing is certain: if you do something new and different consistently and persistently over a period of time, your mind and body adapt. Your comfort zone extends to accommodate your new behaviour as it increasingly becomes *your way*. At times, you'll catch yourself doing it without thinking about it. It's becoming natural to you, *in your muscles*.

Perhaps you've found that some of the methods in this book are familiar and already come naturally to you. They're part of what you already do that works. That's great. **Celebrate your successes daily** (page 159) to recognise, enjoy and deepen your skills in these methods so that you use them more.

Perhaps you've tried other, less familiar methods and had some successes using them but they don't yet come as naturally to you as you would like. The following method gives you ways to build on the daily practice described in **Celebrate your successes daily** to develop your skills in these methods.

Enjoy the journey

The method

Celebrate your successes daily (page 159) describes taking 5 minutes every day to **be impressed... with you!** You can build your confidence and self-esteem as a parent by regularly recalling times when you did a good job. At least three recent examples per day are recommended.

Adapt and extend this daily practice to develop your skills in a particular method as follows:

Preparation:

Choose one method that you want to become more skilled or *natural* at using.

Get really familiar with this method. Read it through several times and identify the key elements that grab you.

Recall any times when you've used the method. Notice the results you got:

- When did it work well?
- When not so well?

Identify any ways to help remind yourself of the key elements of the method as you go about your day, for example, put up sticky notes, put reminders into your mobile phone or ask an understanding friend or partner to remind you at key moments.

Practice:

Keep the method in mind as you go through your day. Notice when and how it is relevant to what's going on. Watch others to see if they're using this method.

Celebrate your successes daily and focus on the method you're practising. Find at least three examples of when you:

- used the method, or bits of it. What results did you get?
- saw things differently as a result of having the method in mind.

Well done for trying or thinking something different.

- When did it work well?
- When not so well?

Enjoy the journey

Practise your chosen method in this way for ten days or so. It's OK to miss a day or two; things are bound to happen that will disrupt your practice. Be kind to yourself and pick up again as soon as you can. Remember that any practice is good practice.

Assess your progress and continue practising until you're happy with your level of skill and the results you're getting using the method.

It's generally best to practise one method at a time, so that you can explore what works for you. If you use several methods at once, it may not be clear which bits are getting good results *for you*. However, practise and develop *your* use of methods as works best for you. And of course this doesn't stop you using other methods as appropriate throughout your day.

Two methods that it's great to practise on an ongoing basis are **Calm down** (page 145) and **Give yourself a good talking to** (page 163). Make these a regular part of your daily practice so that you become very familiar with being calm and hearing your Inner Best Friend encouraging and supporting you. Building your inner resources in this way enables you to stay calmer and more positive during challenging times.

Here's an example:

Preparation:

Choose the method you want to become more skilled or natural at using.

*I often find myself thinking negatively about my kids and complain about them to my friends. I want to try to change this so I will practise the **Clean up your thinking** method (page 111).*

Get really familiar with this method. Read it through several times and identify the key elements that grab you.

The key elements that strike me are:
- *"Everything anyone does has an underlying positive intention."*
- *Ask my kids, "What are you trying to do?", even if I think it's something bad…*

Enjoy the journey

Recall any times when you've used the method. Notice the results you got. When did it work well? When not so well?

On holiday, I enjoyed seeing the kids have fun together. I got to thinking they weren't so bad after all. This put me in a better mood and I was more patient with them.

Identify any ways to remind yourself about the key elements of the method as you go about your day.

I've written: "What's the positive intention?" and "What are you trying to do?" on my hand.

Practice:

Keep the method in mind as much as you can as you go through your day. Notice when and how it is relevant to what's going on.

The writing on my hand has made a big difference – see next step.

Celebrate your successes daily and focus on the method you're practising. Find at least three examples of when you:

- **used the method, or bits of it. What results did you get?**
- **saw things differently as a result of having the method in mind.**

Day 1: *Wow! I've really held back today. I've been much more thoughtful when I would otherwise have "pitched in" at all the usual flashpoints: breakfast, getting washed and dressed, getting out the house, etc. The writing on my hand has helped remind me to notice my thinking and has kind of "come between" me and the situation I'm in. The kids do actually get on with things in their own way …*

Day 2: *Today, I "pitched in" and made things a lot worse. The writing had washed off my hand and I was back to normal, being negative. But I don't want this to be my "normal". I want to be more positive so I've written "What's the positive intention?" and "What are you trying to do?" on my hand again ready for tomorrow…*

Day 3: *I actually noticed the kids doing useful things today: talking nicely, asking politely for pudding, getting half dressed themselves. I felt more positive about them. They're smart and full of energy. I'm checking out the **EASY** method (page 51) to try being impressed with them …*

Day 6: *Today, I met with a friend. We would normally have a good moan about our kids. I did a bit and then realised how I was talking them down. I felt embarrassed so I stopped. It felt odd but good to be more loyal to my kids ...*

Day 10: *Can't believe how much more positive my thinking is about my kids. I'm also giving them more praise using **EASY**. I don't write on my hand every day now but my hand still kind of pops up to remind me to look for the positive.*

Practise the method in this ways for ten days or so. Continue until you're happy with your level of skill and the results you're getting using the method.

I'd like to practise a different method now. Maybe ***Be impressed ... with you!*** (page 153) because I'm making such a difference by ***cleaning up my thinking*** (page 111).

Tips for good results

✓ It's natural to feel strange when trying something different. Try brushing your teeth with your other hand and see how weird that feels! Change often feels uncomfortable at first because you are moving beyond your comfort zone. Sticking with the method you are practising will extend your comfort zone.

✓ Kids are really good at moving beyond their comfort zone and they just keep going until they've mastered something. See the "Have a go" example in **It's cool to copy!** (page 196) for inspiration. Be inspired to have a go yourself and use this method to keep going!

✓ The longer you practise a method, the more natural it will become. Some methods you'll adopt easily and they'll quickly go "into your muscles", whilst others take longer and need more effort. Commit to practising a method for ten days initially, so that you get a sense of how this method works for you.

Enjoy the journey

Trust your judgement and experiences as you practise a method. As long as you're still seeing significant and useful changes, stick with it. As progress levels off, move on to another method.

✓ Practising one method will often lead you to the next method you want to focus on, as shown in the **How this method worked for** … section that follows on page 215. Over time, refresh your memory and skills by checking back and recapping methods you've already practised.

✓ If, after some practice, there are still some aspects of a method that don't quite seem to work for you, that's fine. Just focus on what is working for you and go with that.

✓ Resist the temptation to judge whether your practice is proving useful based on the results of one particular day. Results will vary across different days: on some days you may get some great results, whilst on others you may wonder why you are bothering. Just keep practising and tune in to notice the benefits by **celebrating your successes daily** (Page 159).

Sometimes your practice may not seem particularly inspiring or life changing. However, over time, it can make a profound difference to your life, just like cleaning your teeth maintains your dental health. Also, like cleaning your teeth, when you have established a regular daily practice for a reasonable period of time, you will certainly notice the difference if you miss it for a few days… the equivalent of "yucky teeth"!

✓ By trying something different, you will get new information and a different result. It may not always be useful or what you were expecting. Making mistakes is a vital part of learning so take the learning and move on.

✓ When you're not sure what to make of a situation or experience, use the **How was it for you?** method (page 201) to come to a more helpful understanding.

✓ Practise methods that are familiar to you to deepen your skills and enjoy

Enjoy the journey

the benefits of working to your strengths. Practise other less familiar methods to increase your repertoire and flexibility. This will also increase your awareness of what perhaps comes more naturally to other people. How do they do what they do? It may be **cool to copy** them (page 193).

✓ If you already have a regular daily practice of some sort, that's fantastic – well done! Whether it's physical exercise, yoga or your religious or spiritual practice, consider how you could usefully incorporate ideas from this book into your existing practice.

Now you have a go

Oddly enough, the key to practising anything is to do it regularly! It is this steady input over time that produces lasting changes. You know what to do now so choose your method and go to it!

And finally...

Over time, you will integrate the various skills you have learned through practising different methods. The methods will increasingly become *your way* as you are less consciously aware of what you're doing unless you stop to think about it. You'll also be unconsciously mixing and matching different methods to suit the situation. When you catch yourself doing this, you can be even more impressed with your competence and really proud of the difference this makes to you and your family!

How this method worked for...

John

*The **Get a "Yes!"** method (page 45) really appealed to me. The key element that struck me was getting my daughter to look beyond the task and focus on the benefits of getting it done. It really appealed to her too. Using this method had the immediate effect of making our lives and our relationship much easier and smoother, especially in the morning. We now have lots of fun getting the mundane stuff done, keeping our focus on what we're aiming for beyond the task.*

*I really enjoyed the discipline of focusing on my successes using **Get a "Yes!"** for ten days. By the end, the method was so much part of my thinking that I realised I wanted*

Enjoy the journey

to move on to something else. Practising **Get a "Yes!"** had made me much more aware of how often I said "No". So I read up on **Turning Stop's into Go's** (page 33) in order to find ways of saying "Yes" more often myself. The key element I picked up from this method was to ask myself, "How can I say Yes to this?" whenever I was about to say "No".

Practising this method again had an immediately good effect on our daily lives and relationship. As well as being able to offer more appropriate times and places for my child's requests and undesirable behaviours, I also felt less irritated by them and by her! I continue to enjoy the benefits of focusing my efforts through regular practice.

Result!

Alison

I really wanted to be calmer in my relationships with my children and home life. I decided to practise peripheral vision from the **Calm down** method (page 149). I committed to getting up ten minutes earlier every morning for ten days to **celebrate my successes daily** (page 159) and practise peripheral vision. After a couple of days, I started to get the hang of peripheral vision. I then found I could focus on my breathing, releasing tension and giving me a warm feeling in my body. It seemed a bit weird at first but I stuck to my commitment.

I was really surprised at the effect this had on me. I became much more aware of how tension builds in my body. When I noticed this happening and made a conscious effort to use peripheral vision to calm down, many more useful things seemed to happen! Instead of rushing in and taking over as I had habitually done before, I was able to stay open to other options occurring to me that kind of "unfolded" in the moment…

This inspired me to continue practising calmness and to try practising other methods. **Pause for thought** (page 139) gave me more ways to notice opportunities to not rush in! I then wanted to know more about what I did want to happen so I moved on to practise **What you focus on is what you get** (page 83). I continue to really value my practice time in the morning before anyone else is awake.

Result!

Moments of choice

This book started out by suggesting that, with methods that work and a little practice, you only need a moment, a **pause for thought**, to then choose to:

- Say or do something useful
- Encourage behaviour that you **do** want: behaviour that is positive and useful for you and your children.

The four sections in this book have given you methods to change your **behaviour,** your **thinking**, your **mood** and your **approach to learning** in order to get more of the results you want for yourself and your children. The more you use these methods to tackle the challenges in *your* family life, the more effective *your* pauses for thought will be.

As a result, you will no longer be trapped in patterns of behaviour that don't work – although, for all kinds of reasons, you may still from time to time choose to follow this *downward spiral*. Instead, you can change your response to a situation as it unfolds in real time. Whenever you notice that your response isn't working, this moment becomes a **moment of choice** for you: an opportunity to use something from your *Happy Kids Happy You* toolkit to better effect.

Whether it's turning a don't into a do, taking calm time out to gain a new perspective, planning your day off or simply enjoying the sound of your children's laughter, your efforts to **do**, **think**, **be** and **learn** something different positively reinforce and build on each other. They create an *upward spiral*, leading to different, more useful experiences, greater flexibility and personal resourcefulness. Conversely, continuing to do what you know doesn't work puts you on a *downward spiral*, bringing you more of those familiar results that you don't want.

upward spiral: reinforcing different, more useful results

downward spiral: reinforcing the same results that aren't useful

So stay on your toes and keep your toolkit of methods up to date and well oiled! A well stocked toolkit and the flexibility to switch methods as you need to are the essence of **Happy Kids Happy You**. The more methods you know, the more choices you have to change your approach to create solutions that work *for you*.

And whatever happens, there is always another moment of choice! It's never too late to change tack: to choose to **do**, **think**, **be** or **learn** something different, something more useful, to get better results for you and your children.

Stephen Fischbacher (2002) gives children an idea of **moments of choice** in his song *Build Up*:

Every word you say
Every game you play
Every silly face
Every single place
You can build up, 1, 2, 3, 4, 5... or you can tear down.

Every joke you tell
Every name you spell
Everywhere you go
Everyone you know
You can build up, 1, 2, 3, 4, 5... or you can tear down.

Build up one another
Build up your sisters and brothers
Build up one another
Build up.

The journey continues ...

From one parent to another...

Having read this book and used the methods, you may be wondering how you can share these ideas. Sharing *what works* with others is a great way to **be impressed** (pages 51 and 153) with each other and contribute to everyone's well-being.

It's fascinating to find out how others have tackled challenges. It's inspiring and informative to hear of the strategies and solutions that have worked for them and their children. It's also reassuring to know that you are not alone in the challenges you face: others have "been there, done that" too.

In sharing your experiences you are offering a gift to others, for them to take or leave as they wish. When you recount stories of situations you've handled well, tips and ideas that got you great results, then not only will you feel confident, but you will also be contributing to an upward spiral to **bring out the best in all the parents you know and all the children they care for**.

Here are some suggestions for how you can do this.

Share what works

The methods in this book have been designed for you to try them out and practise them on your own. But there is no reason why you shouldn't have a go at using them with your friends or with your partner. In that way, more people benefit and it's a lot more fun. Bouncing ideas off each other builds confidence and creativity. Listening supportively to each other adds another level of acknowledgement and inspiration. You'll find yourselves coming up with more ideas and having more potential solutions to choose from.

Tips for exploring methods with a friend or partner:

✓ Work through a method with one person guiding the other through the steps and asking them the specific questions. Once the explorer has found a way forward that they are comfortable with, swap roles and you can find another way forward!

✓ Encourage and support each other through the steps of the method as you make discoveries about yourselves and your children.

✓ **Be impressed** with each other: at your intentions to find new, more useful ways forward and your determination to try different things.

✓ As the guide, your role is to hold the framework of the method so that your friend is free to explore within it. Although you might think it helpful to offer advice or recount "similar" experiences as your friend explores, resist the temptation to voice these or to try to "fix" the explorer's problem. Keep the faith that they can and will find a way forward that will work *for them*.

It is OK to share your thoughts *if* the explorer specifically asks for them and *if* you think they may be helpful. And you can of course chat and discuss any relevant experiences you have had *after* they have finished working through the method.

Sharing with a group of friends

The more people you share with, the more ideas you'll get! ***Happy Kids Happy You*** practice groups and workshops provide a safe and supportive environment for practising methods and sharing what works with others. For more information on workshops, practice groups, events and community, and how you can contribute, check out the website

www.happykids-happyyou.co.uk

And you can **share these methods with your children** too! *What works* is no secret:

Matthew

My 4-year-old daughter was busy colouring in a Christmas tree picture but I needed to do some reading with her for school. So I sat down beside her and commented on how lovely her colouring in was. I told her it reminded me of a bedtime story we were reading about Christmas and asked her if she would like to read with me. I got a "Yes!" and we started reading together. After a few minutes, she stopped, looked at me and said, in a matter of fact kind of way, "Daddy, you distracted me didn't you?" I agreed with her and asked if she wanted to go back to her colouring or continue reading with me. She said it was OK to read so we carried on enjoying reading together.

Result!

Being open about what you're doing doesn't detract from its magic. Quite the opposite! What could be more important than passing on methods and skills for communicating more effectively to your children? What could be more satisfying than reaping the benefits here and now for yourselves and your children knowing that, through your children, these skills will be passed on to future generations?

The next stage

A journey of a thousand miles begins with a single step.

Confucius, the Chinese philosopher

When I was expecting our first child, I was chatting with a friend at work about becoming a parent. He had a young family himself and he told me about a conversation he'd had with his Mum not long after he'd become a parent and was finding it tough going. He had asked her which stage she had found most challenging as a parent, when she was bringing him up.

He described how his mother fell silent, apparently lost in thought, reviewing his past. After a few moments, which felt like an eternity to him, she looked him in the eye and said, **"The next one…"**

Parenting is indeed a journey of a thousand miles, with each day a single step and many unknowns along the way. Every moment of every day can become a **moment of choice**: an opportunity for you to bring out the best in yourself and the children you care for, confident that your best is good enough.

Parenting is an extraordinary journey. It means:

- creating and maintaining a space within which another person can grow and develop

- developing a deep and trusting relationship with that person as their personality is forming

- rediscovering and re-connecting with your own childlike learning abilities

- revisiting, reliving, and perhaps re-evaluating your own childhood memories along the way.

This is a journey of extremes, contrasts and opposites. You will encounter:

- powerful emotions, from acute frustration, to exquisite pain, to deep love and lasting joy!

- your ability to trust yourself to look after your children, and then to trust others to look after them and ultimately to trust them to look after themselves!

- that *dance* of responsibility: from the intense, sometimes overwhelming involvement of those early months, through many layers and stages of "letting go" so that you may find yourselves again in the coming together of independent minds.

The challenge of parenting is also its gift. It is the ability to engage, moment by moment, with the wonder and potential that your child brings to the world. In so doing, you are touched by their life force: a force that calls you to be present, to discover and realise the potential in yourself.

Go well!

Appendices

Appendix I

Quick reference guide

This appendix gives suggestions on which method to start with for some common types of challenge. Remember there are no right answers; only what works for you at this time. While the methods will give you something useful in most situations, use what you find works best for you and your children. Be sure to check out **how the methods worked for** others at the end of each method.

References to specific behaviours can be found via the **index**.

Type of challenge	Where to start	Page
My children won't do as I say	Turn Don'ts into Do's	27
	Turn Stop's into Go's	33
My children ignore me	Get down to their level	59
	Join them in their activity	69
Challenging behaviour:		
disruptive	Turn Don'ts into Do's	27
unacceptable	Turn Stop's into Go's	33
inappropriate e.g. shouting	Set and maintain	89
biting, throwing	reasonable boundaries	
confrontational	Move beside	63
provocative	Set and maintain	89
	reasonable boundaries	
winding me up	Find out what your body knows	125
really getting to me	Clean up your thinking	111
doing my head in		
My child is a nightmare	Clean up your thinking	111

Type of challenge	Where to start	Page
Flashpoints/nightmare times of day, e.g. bedtime, mealtimes, leaving, arriving	Pause for thought	139
	What you focus on is what you get	83
	Set and maintain reasonable boundaries	89
	Clean up your thinking	111
Coping with the mess children make	Find a useful meaning	103
	Adjust your expectations	177
	Set and maintain reasonable boundaries	89
Feeling embarrassed/ humiliated by my child's behaviour	Find a useful meaning	103
	How was it for you?	201
	Adjust your expectations	177
Separation anxiety/clingy child	Get a "Yes!"	45
	Get down to their level	59
	How was it for you?	201
Focusing on the negatives about my child all the time	Clean up your thinking	111
	Find a useful meaning	103
	Adjust your expectations	177
Motivating children:		
routine tasks, participating in activities, e.g. eating, dressing, swimming, dancing, football	Offer effective choices	39
	Get a "Yes!"	45
	Set and maintain reasonable boundaries	89
	Give and take: the *dance* of responsibility	97

Type of challenge	Where to start	Page
Building my child's self-esteem, capabilities and confidence, e.g. walking, talking, reading, activities	Be impressed! Give praise the *EASY* way	51
	Give and take: the *dance* of responsibility	97
	What you focus on is what you get	83
Spending "quality time" with my child	Join them in their activity	69
	Be impressed! Give praise the *EASY* way	51
	It's cool to copy!	193
Children comparing and competing with each other	It's cool to copy!	193
Parents comparing and competing with each other	Set and maintain reasonable boundaries	89
	Balance your needs into the mix	171
Doing things I know don't work	Pause for thought	139
	What you focus on is what you get	83
	All the methods in Section 1: go back to basics	23
Overly controlling, taking over what my child is doing	Pause for thought	139
	Give and take: the *dance* of responsibility	97

Type of challenge	Where to start	Page
Letting my children get away with things too much	Set and maintain reasonable boundaries	89
	Give and take: the *dance* of responsibility	97
	Be impressed … with *you*!	153
Losing my temper	Pause for thought	139
	Calm down	145
	How was it for you?	201
Highly self-critical/ giving myself a hard time	Give yourself a *good* talking to	163
Losing my identity, overwhelmed by family life and everyone else's needs	Balance your needs into the mix	171
What role model am I presenting to my children?	Walk your talk	185
Building my own self-esteem, skills and confidence	Be impressed… with *you*!	153
	Practice makes permanent	209

Appendix II

More about Neuro-linguistic Programming

Neuro-linguistic programming (NLP) is about finding and sharing what works in human excellence. It gives us tools to *model* success in others: ways of studying real people to discover and emulate the key elements of their success. We can also use NLP to model our own success, coming to a fuller understanding of what works for us, so we can do it more and share it with others as appropriate. Where others have already modelled excellence in a particular area, we can try out the methods and approaches they have come up with to develop our own abilities.

NLP originated in the 1970s when Richard Bandler and John Grinder studied three outstanding therapists, psychotherapist Fritz Perls, family therapist Virginia Satir and hypnotherapist Milton Erickson. Bandler and Grinder (1975) developed their findings into their own "meta-model for therapy", which became the beginnings of NLP.

Since its emergence, many people have used NLP to model outstanding human endeavours, particularly in the areas of effective communication and relationships. There is a corresponding richness in methods and approaches available to us in these areas. The methods in this book are all based on NLP in one way or another, through the application of existing NLP approaches or my own NLP modelling work. I acknowledge the work of others that has informed my development of *Happy Kids Happy You*, as detailed in the Acknowledgements and in **Appendix III – References and further reading**.

For some suggestions on further NLP-related reading, see the NLP section in **Appendix III**.

Appendix III

References and further reading

This appendix gives a list of key resources that have informed my development of **Happy Kids Happy You**. I have included other references as possible starting points, should you wish to explore further.

Parenting
Andreas, C (1992) *Successful Parenting. An audio cassette programme* Colorado: NLP Comprehensive
Hear an NLP master at work in the field of parenting.

Buxton, J (1998) *Ending the Mother War* London: Macmillan
Explores the pressures of motherhood versus career.

Fischbacher, S (2002) *Build Up: 10 Exciting New Songs on Self-esteem, Bullying and Friendship* (CD and song book) Edinburgh: Fischy Music
Catchy songs for children (and adults!) with great lyrics for building self-esteem.

Martyn, E (2001) *Babyshock! Your Relationship Survival Guide* London: Vermilion
Acknowledging and coping with the impact of the arrival of children on your relationship.

NLP
Andreas, C & Andreas, S (1989) *Heart of the Mind* Utah: Real People Press
A self-help book of NLP techniques applied to specific problems.

Bandler, R & Grinder, J (1975) *The Structure of Magic: A Book About Language and Therapy* California: Science and Behaviour Books
Classic text from the originators of NLP.

Dilts, R & Delozier, J (2000) *Encyclopaedia of NLP* [online] Available at www.nlpuniversitypress.com [accessed 4 Jan 2009]
Limited free access to a comprehensive reference resource, written by two of the original co-developers of NLP.

Gilligan, S (1997) *The Courage to Love: Principles and Practices of Self-relations Psychology* New York: Norton
A powerful mix of Eriksonian hypnosis and Eastern practices.

Gordon, D (1978) *Therapeutic Metaphors* California: Meta Publications Inc.
How to construct a story with a healing message.

Gordon, D & Dawes, G (2005) *Expanding Your World*. David Gordon
A comprehensive guide to modelling with NLP.

Lawley, J & Tompkins, P (2000) *Metaphors in Mind: Transformation through Symbolic Modelling* London: The Developing Company Press
Using "clean language" to explore how we think in symbols and metaphors.

O'Connor, J (2001) *NLP Workbook: A Practical Guide to Achieving the Results you Want* London: Element
All the major NLP approaches and methods.

Personal change and development

Black, J (1994) *Mindstore. The Ultimate Mental Fitness Programme* London: Thorsons
Positive thinking in action through daily practice. A really practical approach with a great section on self-talk and making affirmations.

Covey, S R (1989) *The 7 Habits of Highly Effective People* London: Simon & Schuster
Another useful text on the power of positive thinking with practical tools and techniques to practise regularly.

Johnson, S (2003) *The Present – The Secret to Enjoying Your Work and Life, Now!* London: Bantam Books
An inspirational tale about living in the present moment.

Zander, R S, & Zander, B (2000) *The Art of Possibility: Transforming Professional and Personal Life* Boston: Harvard Business School Press
An inspirational book which offers a set of practices designed to "initiate a new approach to current conditions, based on uncommon assumptions about the nature of the world".

Acknowledgements

I would like to thank

- my children, for providing the continuing challenge, motivation and inspiration for *Happy Kids Happy You*

- all the parents who have contributed to this book by sharing what worked for them so that I can share it with you. Please note that some names have been changed to protect privacy

- my husband Hugh, for making it possible for me to write this book through his tremendous patience, encouragement and support

- my parents, wider family and friends for their encouragement and support

- my "co-conspirator" Adam Crisp, for his energy, ideas and faith in *Happy Kids Happy You*

- my proofreaders Heather Clark-Kelly, Jackie Drake and my sister Bev Davies for their invaluable and timely input

- my coach Garry Cook, for helping me find the way

- my NLP trainers and mentors, for sharing their skills, insights and enthusiasm. I would especially like to thank

  - Judith Delozier, for her faith and support in this project

  - Connirae Andreas, for her inspiring work in the field of parenting

  - Stephen Gilligan, whose work I refer to on a daily basis

  - Fran Burgess and Derek Jackson at the Northern School of NLP, for bringing leading international NLP co-developers and trainers to the north of England

  - Andy Smith, for an inspiring and comprehensive introduction to NLP

- everyone at Crown House Publishing, for helping to bring *Happy Kids Happy You* to a wider audience.

Index

Index

practice, daily *209, 210, 211, 214, 215, 236*

praise, effective *51, 56, 91, 107, 142, 155, 178*

punishment *93*

R

reflection *81, 107, 161, 179, 201, 202, 205, 206*

relationships *12, 20, 71, 81, 89, 93, 102, 130, 137, 169, 216, 233*

relaxation *145*

resentment *193, 195*

resistance *36, 39, 46*

respect *43, 46, 62, 75, 77, 110, 130, 141, 193*

response, immediate *104-110, 133, 178*

responsibility *39, 90, 97-102*

   collective *178*

   giving *99, 101*

   level of *98, 100, 101*

   taking *66, 97-102*

rewards *93, 159, 162, 174*

role model(s) *141, 158, 188, 190, 197, 231*

routine tasks *42, 45, 48, 229*

rudeness *67, 111, 207*

rules (see also house rules) *89, 92, 94, 105*

S

satisfaction, personal *169*

school *45, 47, 62, 70, 92, 109, 110, 133, 166, 223*

self-talk *84, 236*

self-esteem *51, 56, 153, 158, 230, 231*

self-worth *158, 169*

separation anxiety, *see* clingy behaviour

Set and maintain reasonable boundaries (method) *16, 31, 60, 81, 89-95, 100, 188, 208, 229, 330, 232*

shouting *20, 34, 35, 77, 92, 94, 145, 228*

sleep deprivation *123*

spitting *35*

stepping back *97-101, 141, 183*

stepping in *97-101, 128, 131, 174*

stuckness *125, 134, 150, 168, 201, 206, 216*

success(es) *55, 137, 153, 155, 159-161, 174, 209, 210, 214-216, 233*

swimming *36, 94*

T

tantrum(s) *132, 139, 161, 193, 195, 204*

television *168*

"the turn" *66, 67*

thinking *12, 16, 28, 79, 82-85, 107, 108, 111, 113, 114, 117, 119-122, 125, 126, 128, 130, 131, 133, 134, 137, 141, 147, 149, 150-152, 154, 163, 173, 180, 188, 190, 194, 197, 202, 205-207, 209-213, 215, 217, 228, 229*

   control your *145, 147*

   negative *111, 113, 114, 117, 118, 122*

   positive *85, 119*

thoughts, positive *111*

throwing *19, 21, 35, 195, 228*

tidiness *54, 67, 85, 87, 177, 178*

time

   one-to-one *74*

   spending more (with children) *73*

toileting *87*

Praise for *Happy Kids Happy You*

Sue's book arrived at a perfect time for me. I was at a low point in my life; job worries, financial worries, my children were grumpy and shouting at me – I was grumpy and shouting at them, and my partner and I weren't even talking to each other! I was aware that something needed to change but wasn't sure what or how... I read Sue's book and realised that I needed to "clean up my thinking", "pause for thought", "give myself (and my partner) a good talking to", because "what you focus on is want you get". Just taking time out to read the book gave me valuable time to think about myself as a parent (and a partner) and about how I interact with my family.

I always thought that I was quite a calm person until I had kids, but they seem to be able to push all my red buttons and I can lose my temper with them like I never thought I could. The "calm down" and "pause for thought" methods really helped me as this then gives me space to make a choice to change my reaction and to come up with a more useful one. For example, my 4-year-old was doing her usual routine of making a fuss about getting dressed in the morning to go out to preschool. Usually, her defiant "No" would make me feel cross and the situation would then spiral into disaster, resulting in me losing my temper and my daughter getting upset and more defiant! Not a good way to start the day! At the first "No" I decided to pause for thought and told her that I was leaving the room to go and do something else more useful than standing around and shouting. "But then I won't be able to get dressed with you" came her reply. "OK" I said, "Come here then and I'll help you get dressed calmly and happily." So much better for all of us! I felt so proud of both of us for making the choice to change the situation.

"Clean up your thinking" made me challenge my negative thinking about my children, and after using the "assume an underlying positive intention" method, I have successfully dealt with several blossoming arguments between my children. My eldest loves to draw and finds her younger sister quite annoying when she's involved in creating a masterpiece (I know this because she often tells her how annoying she is!). I looked for her positive intention and she replied that her sister always made a mess on her pictures. I asked her to find a pen and some paper for her sister, which she did, and even began to show her how to draw a cat! So simple, but just by assuming that she didn't actually want to hurt her sister, that she was just protecting her artwork, calmness and cooperation was quickly restored.

Happy Kids Happy You has inspired me to think more usefully for myself, and opened up my mind to new ways of seeing my children and their behaviour. I found "it's cool to copy" really interesting as I had generally seen copying as a negative thing and had discouraged my children from doing it, but I now see this as a compliment and also a way to learn more, to become curious myself!

Sue assumes that we already know how to be good parents, and the book is a guide to being a better parent – being kinder to yourself and your family, which is so simple, yet we don't always know how to do it. The book is a gentle toolkit of methods which are easy to follow and easy to recall when you're in the middle of a potentially difficult situation. The Appendix is extremely helpful as a quick reference guide and my copy is already well thumbed!

Emma Golden
Parent from Oldham

++++

In my opinion, raising our children is the most joyful, demanding and valuable thing we will ever do and as parents we can never get enough reassurance that we are on the right track in our parenting, as well as getting some practical advice on how to do this better. By suggesting positive, lateral ways of managing confrontation with our children, this book offers positive and alternative approaches that have a real ring of truth and humour, challenging with a light touch.

Happy Kids Happy You provides wise, sensible, often amusing insights into managing not just our children but ourselves. Through simple, attainable exercises, helpful illustrations that are often painfully funny and numerous examples of positive ways to deal with our children and our "own stuff", Sue Beever has come up trumps with this excellent resource for anyone serious about not just their children's well-being but also their own emotional health.

Stephen Fischbacher
Creative Director, Fischy Music

Happy Kids Happy You by Sue Beever is a great gift to the world. Sue's book offers ideas and tools on many levels for assisting in the hardest job that most of us do in life, raise children. This book will produce more happiness in the family through helping us be better guides, mentors and sponsors of our children's growth.

Judith Delozier
Delozier and Associates International

++++

Happy Kids Happy You is a fascinating book in which Sue takes the complex workings of children and steers the reader gently through the minefield of managing their behaviour!

A cross between a workshop manual and advice from your favourite agony aunt, Sue manages to balance gentle nurturing and coaxing with a serious dose of "beware and defuse".

Anyone who is responsible for the emotional development and welfare of young children should buy this book!

It is easy as adults for us to hide behind the belief that "the adult is always right". Using tried and tested NLP techniques Sue challenges you to think about your interactions with young children and how it feels to be on the receiving end of your language, feelings, behaviour and attitude.

This common sense practical guide helps you to re-think and re-programme how you speak to, behave and interact with little ones ensuring a better outcome for you both.

Sue Overton
Founder of Sue Overton Associates

++++

Notes

Notes

Notes

Notes

Notes

Notes

Notes

Notes

Notes